Houghton
Mifflin
Harcourt

CALIFORNIA

MATH

Expressions
Common Core

Dr. Karen C. Fuson

GRADE

5

Volume 2

This material is based upon work supported by the
National Science Foundation
under Grant Numbers
ESI-9816320, REC-9806020, and RED-935373.

Any opinions, findings, and conclusions, or recommendations expressed in this material
are those of the author and do not necessarily reflect the views of the National Science Foundation.

VOLUME 2 CONTENTS

UNIT 5 Division with Whole Numbers and Decimals

BIG IDEA 1   Division with Whole Numbers

1 Divide Whole Numbers by One Digit
5.NBT.6 . . . . **161**

       FAMILY LETTER **161**

2 Explore Dividing by Two-Digit Whole Numbers
5.NBT.6 . . . . **167**

3 Too Large, Too Small, or Just Right?
5.NBT.6 . . . . **169**

4 Interpret Remainders
5.NBT.6 . . . . **171**

5 Division Practice
5.NBT.6 . . . . **175**

BIG IDEA 2   Division with Decimal Numbers

6 Divide Decimal Numbers by Whole Numbers
5.NBT.7 . . . . **177**

7 Divide Whole Numbers by Decimal Numbers
5.NBT.2, 5.NBT.7 . . . . **181**

8 Divide with Two Decimal Numbers
5.NBT.2, 5.NBT.7 . . . . **187**

9 Division Practice
5.NBT.6, 5.NBT.7 . . . . **191**

10 Distinguish Between Multiplication and Division
5.NBT.5, 5.NBT.6, 5.NBT.7, 5.NF.5, 5.NF.5a **193**

11 Focus on Mathematical Practices
5.NBT.7 . . . . **197**

     ✓ **Unit 5 Test** **197**

UNIT 6 Operations and Word Problems

BIG IDEA 1 Equations and Problem Solving

1 Situation and Solution Equations for Addition and Subtraction
5.NBT.7, 5.NF.2 . . . . **205**

    FAMILY LETTER **205**

2 Situation and Solution Equations for Multiplication and Division
5.NBT.5, 5.NBT.6, 5.NBT.7, 5.NF.4, 5.NF.4b, 5.NF.6, 5.NF.7, 5.NF.7c **209**

3 Write Word Problems
5.NF.4a, 5.NF.7a, 5.NF.7b **211**

4 Determine Reasonable Answers
5.NBT.4, 5.NBT.6, 5.NBT.7, 5.NF.1, 5.NF.2 . . . . **213**

BIG IDEA 2 Comparison Word Problems

5 Language of Comparison Problems
5.NBT.5 . . . . **215**

6 Multiplicative Comparison Problems
5.NBT.5, 5.NBT.6, 5.NBT.7, 5.NF.5, 5.NF.5a, 5.NF.5b, 5.NF.6, 5.NF.7c **217**

7 Types of Comparison Problems
5.NBT.5, 5.NBT.6, 5.NBT.7, 5.NF.2 . . . . **219**

BIG IDEA 3 Problems with More Than One Step

8 Equations and Parentheses
5.OA.1, 5.NBT.5 5.NBT.7, 5.NF.2, 5.NF.6, 5.NF.7c **221**

9 Multistep Word Problems
5.NBT.5, 5.NBT.6, 5.NBT.7, 5.NF.2, 5.NF.6 . . . . **225**

10 Practice Problem Solving
5.NBT.6, 5.NF.2, 5.NF.6, 5.NF.7c **227**

11 Focus on Mathematical Practices
5.NBT.7 . . . . **229**

☑ **Unit 6 Test** **231**

UNIT 7 Algebra, Patterns, and Coordinate Graphs

BIG IDEA 1   Algebraic Reasoning and Expressions

1   Read and Write Expressions
5.OA.1, 5.OA.2 .... **237**

    FAMILY LETTER **237**

2   Simplify Expressions
5.OA.1 .... **241**

3   Evaluate Expressions
5.OA.1, 5.OA.2 .... **243**

BIG IDEA 2   Patterns and Graphs

4   Patterns and Relationships
CC5.OA.1, 5.OA.2, 5.OA.2.1, 5.OA.3 .... **245**

5   The Coordinate Plane
CC5.G.1 .... **249**

6   Graph Ordered Pairs
5.OA.3, CC5.G.1, CC5.G.2 .... **253**

7   Focus on Mathematical Practices
CC5.G.1, CC5.G.2 .... **255**

    Unit 7 Test **257**

UNIT 8 Measurement and Geometry

BIG IDEA 1   Measurements and Data

1   Convert Metric Units of Length
5.MD.1 .... **263**

    FAMILY LETTER **263**

2   Metric Units of Liquid Volume
5.MD.1 .... **269**

3   Metric Units of Mass
5.MD.1 .... **271**

4   Customary Units of Length
5.MD.1 .... **273**

5   Customary Measures of Liquid Volume
5.MD.1 .... **275**

6   Customary Units of Weight
5.MD.1 .... **277**

7   Read and Make Line Plots
5.MD.2 .... **279**

VOLUME 2 CONTENTS (continued)

BIG IDEA 2   Area and Volume

8   Perimeter and Area of Rectangles
5.NF.4b **281**

9   Cubic Units and Volume
5.MD.3a, 5.MD.3b, 5.MD.4 . . . . **285**

10   Visualize Volume
5.MD.3, 5.MD.3a, 5.MD.3b **287**

11   Introduce Volume Formulas
5.MD.5a, 5.MD.5b **289**

12   Relate Length, Area, and Volume
5.MD.5b **291**

13   Volume of Composite Solid Figures
5.MD.5, 5.MD.5b, 5.MD.5c **293**

BIG IDEA 3   Classify Geometric Figures

14   Attributes of Quadrilaterals
5.G.3, 5.G.4 . . . . **295**

15   Attributes of Triangles
5.G.3, 5.G.4 . . . . **297**

16   Attributes of Two-Dimensional Shapes
5.G.3, 5.G.4 . . . . **299**

17   **Focus on Mathematical Practices**
5.MD.3, 5.MD.5, 5.MD.5b **301**

☑   **Unit 8 Test** **303**

Student Resources

Table of Measures **S1**

Table of Units of Time and Table of Formulas. **S2**

Properties of Operations and Order of Operations **S3**

Problem Types **S4**

Vocabulary Activities **S10**

Glossary. **S14**

Correlation: California Common Core Standards for Mathematical Content **S25**

Correlation: California Common Core Standards for Mathematical Practice **S30**

Index **S34**

Family Letter

Content Overview

Dear Family,

The main goal of Unit 5 of *Math Expressions* is to enhance skills in dividing with whole numbers and decimal numbers. Some additional goals are:

▶ to solve real world application problems,

▶ to use patterns as an aid in calculating,

▶ to use estimation to check the reasonableness of answers, and

▶ to interpret remainders.

Your child will learn and practice methods such as Place Value Sections, Expanded Notation, and Digit-by-Digit to gain speed and accuracy in multidigit and decimal division. Money examples will be used to help students understand division with decimals.

Throughout Unit 5, your child will solve real world application problems that require multidigit division. Your child will learn to estimate using rounding and other methods, and then to use estimation to determine whether answers are reasonable. Remainders will be interpreted in real world contexts, and expressed as fractions or decimals when appropriate. Students will learn to distinguish between multiplication and division in real world situations involving decimals.

If you have any questions, please call or write to me.

Sincerely,
Your child's teacher

 CA CC

Unit 5 addresses the following standards from the *Common Core State Standards for Mathematics with California Additions*: **5.NBT.2, 5.NBT.5, 5.NBT.6, 5.NBT.7, 5.NF.5, 5.NF.5a,** and all Mathematical Practices.

Estimada familia:

El objetivo principal de la Unidad 5 de *Math Expressions* es reforzar las destrezas de división con números enteros y decimales. Algunos objetivos adicionales son:

▶ resolver problemas con aplicaciones a la vida diaria,

▶ usar patrones como ayuda para hacer cálculos,

▶ usar la estimación para comprobar si las respuestas son razonables, y por último,

▶ interpretar residuos.

Su niño aprenderá y practicará métodos como el de Secciones de valor posicional, Notación extendida y Dígito por dígito, para realizar divisiones de números de varios dígitos y decimales con mayor rapidez y exactitud. Como ayuda para comprender las divisiones con decimales, se usarán ejemplos de dinero.

En la Unidad 5 su niño resolverá problemas con aplicaciones a la vida diaria que requieran el uso de la división de números de varios dígitos. Aprenderá a estimar usando el redondeo y otros métodos, y luego usará la estimación para determinar si las respuestas son razonables. Los residuos se interpretarán dentro de contextos de la vida diaria y se expresarán como fracciones o decimales cuando sea apropiado. Los estudiantes aprenderán a distinguir entre la multiplicación y la división en situaciones de la vida cotidiana que involucren decimales.

Si tiene alguna duda o algún comentario, por favor comuníquese conmigo.

Atentamente,
El maestro de su niño

CA CC

En la Unidad 5 se aplican los siguientes estándares auxiliares, contenidos en los *Estándares estatales comunes de matemáticas con adiciones para california*: **5.NBT.2, 5.NBT.5, 5.NBT.6, 5.NBT.7, 5.NF.5, 5.NF.5a** y todos los de prácticas matemáticas.

Divide Whole Numbers by One Digit

► Compare Division Methods

An airplane travels the same distance every day.
It travels 3,822 miles in a week. How far does the
airplane travel each day?

Rectangle Model

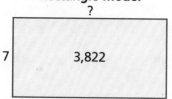

Place Value Sections

500		

```
      500
   ┌───────┐
 7 │ 3,822 │
   │ −3,500│
   └───────┘
      322
```

Build a new
section with
each leftover
amount.

```
      500 + 40
   ┌───────┬──────┐
 7 │ 3,822 │ 322  │
   │ −3,500│ −280 │
   └───────┴──────┘
      322     42
```

```
      500 + 40 + 6 = 546
   ┌───────┬──────┬─────┐
 7 │ 3,822 │ 322  │ 42  │
   │ −3,500│ −280 │ −42 │
   └───────┴──────┴─────┘
      322     42
```

Expanded Notation

```
      500
    ┌──────
 7 )3,822
    −3,500
      322
```

Show the
zeros in the
multipliers.

```
       40
      500
    ┌──────
 7 )3,822
    −3,500
      322
     −280
       42
```

```
        6
       40  ⎤
      500  ⎬ 546
    ┌──────⎦
 7 )3,822
    −3,500
      322
     −280
       42
      −42
```

Digit-by-Digit

```
      5
    ┌──────
 7 )3,822
    −3,5
      32
```

Put in only
one digit at
a time.

```
     54
    ┌──────
 7 )3,822
    −35
      32
     −28
       42
```

```
     546
    ┌──────
 7 )3,822
    −3,5
      32
     −28
       42
      −42
```

▶ Division Problems

Write an equation. Then solve.

Show your work.

1. A farmer has 2,106 cows and 9 barns. If the farmer divides the cows into equal groups, how many cows will he put in each barn?

   _____

2. A sidewalk covers 3,372 square feet. If the sidewalk is 4 feet wide, what is its length?

   ?

   4 ft | Area = 3,372 sq. ft

   _____

3. Olivia has $8. Her mother has $4,784. The amount Olivia's mother has is how many times the amount Olivia has?

   _____

4. A machine produced 4,650 bottles of seltzer and put them in packs of six bottles. How many 6-packs did the machine make?

   _____

5. Raj is 3,288 days old. This is 6 times as old as his niece. How many days old is Raj's niece?

   _____

6. If a streamer is unrolled, its area is 3,888 square inches. If the streamer is 2 inches wide, how long is it?

   _____

Divide Whole Numbers by One Digit

VOCABULARY

dividend   quotient

divisor   remainder

► Work with Remainders

The problem at the right might seem unfinished. The leftover number at the bottom is called the remainder. We can write the answer like this: 567 R2.

```
            567 ←quotient
divisor→ 8)4,538 ←dividend
          −40
           53
          −48
           58
          −56
remainder → 2
```

7. Could there be a remainder of 9 for the problem? Why or why not?

No. If there was a remainder greater then

8. What is the greatest possible remainder when dividing by 8?

Complete each division and give the remainder.

9. 6)5,380

10. 7)6,747

11. 5)4,914 r=4

12. 5)2,428

13. 3)2,972   990 R=2

14. 7)4800 685 R=5

15. 9)5,469

16. 4)3,183

17. 6)5,420

18. 8)6,002

19. 2)3,303

20. 7)4,000

▶ Use Mental Math to Check for Reasonableness

Miguel has 6 boxes to store 1,350 baseball cards.
He divides and finds that each box will have 225 cards.
To check that his answer is reasonable, he uses
estimation and mental math:

$$6\overline{)1{,}350} \quad \overset{225}{}$$

"I know that $1{,}200 \div 6$ is 200 and $1{,}800 \div 6$ is 300.
Because 1,350 is between 1,200 and 1,800, my answer
should be between 200 and 300. It is."

Solve. Then use mental math to check the solution.

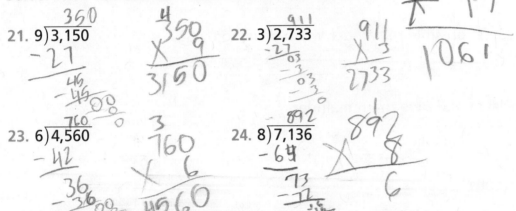

21. $9\overline{)3{,}150}$

22. $3\overline{)2{,}733}$

23. $6\overline{)4{,}560}$

24. $8\overline{)7{,}136}$

25. Kim makes necklaces with colored beads. She used 1,620
    beads for 9 necklaces. How many beads did she use
    for each necklace if they have the same number of beads?

_____

26. Saul delivers equally 1,155 newspapers in a 7-day week.
    How many newspapers does he deliver in a day?

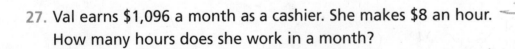

_____

27. Val earns $1,096 a month as a cashier. She makes $8 an hour.
    How many hours does she work in a month?

_____

28. The Martinson School bought 1,890 water bottles to distribute
    equally among students over a 5-day period. How many bottles
    are distributed each day?

_____

Name _____ **Date** _____

CA CC Content Standards **5.NBT.6**
Mathematical Practices **MP.1, MP.3, MP.4, MP.6**

► Experiment with Two-Digit Divisors

Suppose 2,048 sheep are to be sent on a train.
Each railroad car holds 32 sheep.

To find how many railroad cars are needed for the
sheep, divide 2,048 by 32.

Rectangle Model

?
32   2,048

Discuss how these division methods are alike and different.

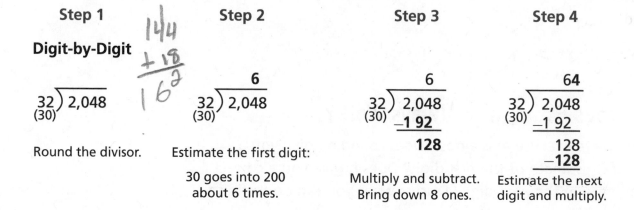

Step 1	**Step 2**	**Step 3**	**Step 4**
Digit-by-Digit			
$32\overline{)2{,}048}$ (30)	$32\overline{)2{,}048}$ (30) — 6	$32\overline{)2{,}048}$ (30) —1 92 = 128 — 6	$32\overline{)2{,}048}$ (30) —1 92 = 128 —128 — 64
Round the divisor.	Estimate the first digit: 30 goes into 200 about 6 times.	Multiply and subtract. Bring down 8 ones.	Estimate the next digit and multiply.

handwritten: 144 + 18 = 162

Expanded Notation			
$32\overline{)2{,}048}$ (30)	$32\overline{)2{,}048}$ (30) — 60	$32\overline{)2{,}048}$ (30) —1,920 = 128 — 60	$32\overline{)2{,}048}$ (30) —1,920 = 128 —128 — 4 } 64, 60
Round the divisor.	Estimate the first number: 30 goes into 2,000 about 60 times.	Multiply and subtract. 60 · 32 = 1,920	Estimate the next number and multiply.

handwritten: 20 ✗

Place Value Sections

60	**60**	**60 +**	**60 + 4**
32 (30) | 2,048	32 (30) | 2,048 —1,920 = 128	32 (30) | 2,048 1,920 | 128 = 128	32 (30) | 2,048 —1,920 | 128 —128 = 128 0
Round the divisor and estimate the first number.	Multiply and subtract.	Make a new section.	Estimate the next number, and multiply and subtract.

*quotient * divisor = dividend* (+R)

▶ Experiment with Two-Digit Divisors (continued)

Look at Exercises 1–3. Would you round the divisor up or
down to estimate the first digit of the quotient?
Complete each exercise, using any method you choose.

1. 79)4,032   51 R 3
   -395
   82
   -79
   3

2. 21)1,533
   50
   ×70
   390

3. 18)1,061   59 R
   -90
   161
   -144
   17

▶ Does Estimation Always Work?

Complete Exercise 4 as a class. Does rounding give you a
correct estimate of the first digit? Does it give you a correct
estimate of the next digit? Discuss what you can do to finish
the problem.

4. 54)3,509   64 R
   -324
   269
   -216
   53

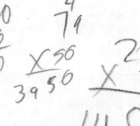

80)4032   80   7 4
          ×6   ×50
          480 3950

20
×70
1400
+20

20
×6
120

Complete and discuss each exercise below. Use any method
you choose.

5. 74)3,651   49 r=25
   -296
   691
   -666
   25

20
×3
60

6. 42)3,231   76 R 39
   -294
   291
   -252
   39

7. 23)1,892   82 r=6
   -184
   052
   -46
   6

Explore Dividing by Two-Digit Whole Numbers

▶ Underestimating

Here are two ways to divide 5,185 ÷ 85. Discuss each method and answer the questions as a class.

$$\begin{array}{r} 5 \\ (90)\,85)\overline{5{,}185} \\ 4\ 25 \\ \hline 93 \end{array}$$

What does this number tell us?

How do we know that the first estimated number is not right? What number should we try next? Solve the problem using that number.

$$\begin{array}{r} 10 \\ 50 \\ (90)\,85)\overline{5{,}185} \\ 4{,}250 \\ \hline 935 \end{array}$$

What does this number tell us?

How do we know that the first estimated number is not right this time? Do we need to erase, or can we just finish solving the problem? Try it.

1. When we estimate with a number that is too big (**overestimate**), we have to erase and change the number. When we estimate with a number that is too small (**underestimate**), do we always have to erase? Explain your answer.

_____

_____

_____

_____

Solve each division. You may need to adjust one or both of the estimated numbers.

2.
$$\begin{array}{r} 72 \\ 56)\overline{4{,}032} \\ -392 \\ \hline 112 \\ -112 \\ \hline 0 \end{array}$$

3.
$$\begin{array}{r} 64 \quad 77 \\ 77)\overline{4{,}791} \\ -442 \\ \hline 371 \\ -308 \\ \hline 63 \end{array}$$

4.
$$\begin{array}{r} 44\,R6 \\ 18)\overline{798} \\ -72 \\ \hline 78 \\ -72 \\ \hline 6 \end{array}$$

Too Large, Too Small, or Just Right? **169**

Name _____ Date _____

▶ Too High or Too Low?

Think about what kind of divisor is most likely to lead to an estimated number that is wrong. Test your idea by doing the first step of each problem below.

5. $41\overline{)2{,}583}$ 6. $34\overline{)1{,}525}$ 7. $29\overline{)928}$ 8. $16\overline{)1{,}461}$

What kind of divisor is most likely to lead to an estimated number that is wrong? How can you adjust for these cases?

in the ones place
the numbers 4 5 & 6

▶ Mixed Practice with Adjusted Estimates

Solve.

Show your work.

10. Hector is packing 1,375 oranges in crates that hold 24 oranges each.

    How many crates will Hector fill? __57__

    How many oranges will be left over? __7__

$$
\begin{array}{r}
24 \\
\times\ 5 \\
\hline
120
\end{array}
$$

$$
\begin{array}{r}
57 \\
24\overline{)1375} \\
-120 \\
\hline
175 \\
-168 \\
\hline
7
\end{array}
$$

$$
\begin{array}{r}
24 \\
\times\ 7 \\
\hline
168
\end{array}
$$

11. Skateboards sell for $76 each. This week the store sold $5,396 worth of skateboards.

    How many skateboards were sold?

    71 skateboards

12. Ashley's dog Tuffy eats 21 ounces of food for each meal. Ashley has 1,620 ounces of dog food.

    How many meals will Tuffy have before Ashley needs to buy more food? __77__

    How many ounces of food will be left after the last meal? __3__

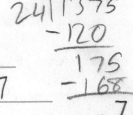

$$
\begin{array}{r}
77\ R3 \\
21\overline{)1620} \\
-147 \\
\hline
150 \\
-147 \\
\hline
3
\end{array}
$$

Too Large, Too Small, or Just Right?

CA CC Content Standards **5.NBT.6**
Mathematical Practices **MP.1, MP.3, MP.6**

Name _____ **Date** _____

▶ Decide What to Do with the Remainder

Think about each of these ways to use a remainder.

Sometimes you ignore the remainder.

1. A roll of ribbon is 1,780 inches long. It takes 1 yard of ribbon (36 inches) to wrap a gift.

   How many gifts can be wrapped?

   49 R16

   Why do you ignore the remainder?

   16 in. can't wrap a gift.

Sometimes you round up to the next whole number.

2. There are 247 people traveling to the basketball tournament by bus. Each bus holds 52 people.

   How many buses will be needed?

   5

   Why do you round up?

   the rest of the people, 39, would be left behind

Sometimes you use the remainder to form a fraction.

3. The 28 students in Mrs. Colby's class will share 98 slices of pizza equally.

   How many slices will each student get?

   $3\frac{1}{2}$

   $$28\overline{)98} \quad 3\frac{1}{2}$$
   $$-84$$
   $$14$$

   Look at the division shown here. Explain how to get the fraction after you find the remainder.

   28 divided by 2 = 14.

▶ Decide What to Do with the Remainder (continued)

Sometimes you use a decimal number instead of the remainder.

Suppose 16 friends earned $348 at a car wash. They want to divide the money equally. The division at the right shows that each friend gets $21, and there are $12 leftover. Dividing the $12, each friend gets an additional $\frac{12}{16}$, or $\frac{3}{4}$, of a dollar, for a total of $21.75.

$$
\begin{array}{r}
21.75 \\
16\overline{)348} \\
-32 \\
\hline
28 \\
16 \\
\hline
12
\end{array}
$$

4. A rectangular garden has an area of 882 square meters. The long side of the garden has a length of 35 meters. How long is the short side?

   25.2 meters

Sometimes the remainder is the answer to the problem.

5. A bagel shop has 138 bagels to be packed into boxes of 12 to be sold. The extra bagels are for the workers.

   How many bagels will the workers get?

   6

   Why is the remainder the answer?

   132 bagels have already been sold, the leftovers/remainders are for the workers.

$$
\begin{array}{r}
11 \\
12\overline{)138} \\
-12 \\
\hline
18 \\
-12 \\
\hline
6
\end{array}
$$

▶ Solve Problems Involving Remainders

Solve.

Show your work.

6. At the Cactus Flower Cafe, all the tips are divided equally among the waiters. Last night, the 16 waiters took in $1,108 in tips. How much did each waiter get?

   _____

7. A gardener needs to move 2,150 pounds of dirt. He can carry 98 pounds in his wheelbarrow. How many trips will he need to make with the wheelbarrow?

Interpret Remainders

► Solve Problems Involving Remainders (continued)

Solve.   *Show your work.*

8. Mia must work 133 hours during the month of May.
   There are 21 working days in May this year. How many
   hours per day will Mia work if she works the same
   number of hours each day?

   _____

9. Colored markers cost 78 cents each. Pablo has $21.63 in
   his pocket. How many markers can Pablo buy?

   _____

10. A meat packer has 180 kilograms of ground meat. He
    will divide it equally into 50 packages. How much will
    each package weigh?

    _____

11. In volleyball, there are 12 players on the court. If
    75 people all want to play volleyball at a gym that has
    more than enough courts, how many of them must sit
    out at one time?

    _____

12. At the Fourth of July celebration, 1,408 ounces of
    lemonade will be shared equally by 88 people. How
    many ounces of lemonade will each person get?

    _____

13. Armando needs quarters to ride the bus each day. He
    took $14.87 to the bank and asked to have it changed
    into quarters. How many quarters did he get?

    _____

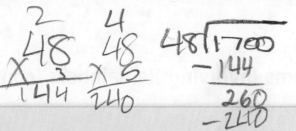

► What's the Error?

Dear Math Students,

I am moving, and I need to pack my sardines.
I have 1,700 cans of sardines, and I know I
can fit 48 cans in each box.

I divided to figure out how many boxes I
needed. I bought 35 boxes, but I had some
cans leftover. What did I do wrong?

Your friend,
Puzzled Penguin

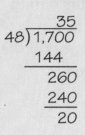

```
        35
48)1,700
    144
    260
    240
     20
```

14. Write a response to Puzzled Penguin.

_____

_____

_____

_____

► Write Your Own Problem

15. Write a word problem that involves a division that has
a remainder. Solve your problem and explain what
you did with the remainder in your solution.

_____

_____

_____

_____

Name _____ **Date** _____

CA CC Content Standards **5.NBT.6**
Mathematical Practices **MP.1, MP.6**

▶ Practice Dividing

Divide.

1. $6\overline{)546}$
   $\begin{array}{r} 91 \\ \hline -54 \\ \hline 06 \\ -6 \\ \hline 0 \end{array}$

2. $43\overline{)1,634}$

3. $5\overline{)423}$ R3
   $\begin{array}{r} 84 \\ \hline +40 \\ \hline 23 \\ -20 \end{array}$

4. $73\overline{)3,942}$

5. $5\overline{)7,016}$
   $\begin{array}{r} 140 \\ \hline 5 \\ \hline 20 \\ -20 \\ \hline 90 \\ -16 \end{array}$

6. $55\overline{)2,200}$

7. $13\overline{)9,430}$
   725
   $\begin{array}{r} -91 \\ \hline 33 \\ -26 \\ \hline 70 \\ -65 \\ \hline 9 \end{array}$
   $\begin{array}{r} 13 \\ \times 7 \\ \hline 91 \end{array}$
   $\begin{array}{r} 13 \\ \times 5 \\ \hline 65 \end{array}$
   $\begin{array}{r} 13 \\ \times 2 \\ \hline 20 \end{array}$

8. $29\overline{)1,499}$

9. $3\overline{)4,040}$ R2
   $\begin{array}{r} 1346 \\ \hline -3 \\ \hline 10 \\ -9 \\ \hline 14 \\ -12 \\ \hline 28 \\ -18 \\ \hline 2 \end{array}$

10. $8\overline{)2,007}$
    $\begin{array}{r} 25 \\ \hline -16 \\ \hline 40 \\ -40 \\ \hline 01 \end{array}$

11. $88\overline{)6,160}$

12. $76\overline{)3,441}$

13. $41\overline{)3,605}$
    $\begin{array}{r} 87 \\ \hline -328 \\ \hline 325 \\ -287 \\ \hline 38 \end{array}$
    $\begin{array}{r} 41 \\ \times 8 \\ \hline 328 \end{array}$
    $\begin{array}{r} 41 \\ \times 7 \\ \hline 287 \end{array}$

14. $19\overline{)6,000}$

15. $28\overline{)8,413}$

▶ Solve Division Word Problems

Solve.

Show your work.

16. The Thomas's rectangular backyard has an area of
    2,352 square feet. If the yard is 56 feet long, how wide is it?

    _____

17. Milo wants to make guacamole for a party. Avocados
    are on sale for 84¢ each. How many avocados can Milo
    buy if he has $7.75?

    _____

18. One quart is equal to 32 ounces. How many quarts are
    equal to 6,672 ounces?

    _____

19. Students in the marching band sold calendars to raise
    money for new uniforms. Violet sold 24 calendars for a
    total of $186. How much did each calendar cost?

    _____

20. Only 37 fans came to watch the volleyball team's first match.
    At the last match, 2,035 fans came to watch. The number
    of fans at the last match was how many times the
    number at the first?

    _____

21. Ayala has 655 computer files she wants to put on CDs.
    If she can fit 18 files on each CD, how many CDs will she need?

    _____

22. Ms. Adams wrote a 36-page short story that she wants to
    send to publishers. She buys a 500-sheet package of paper
    and prints as many copies of the story as she can. How many
    sheets does she have left over?

    _____

Division Practice

Name _____ Date _____

CA CC Content Standards **5.NBT.7**
Mathematical Practices **MP.1, MP.4, MP.6, MP.7, MP.8**

► Divide a Decimal by a One-Digit Number

Three friends set up a lemonade stand and made $20.25.
They will share the money equally. Study the steps below to see
how much money each person should get.

When the $20 is split 3 ways, each person gets $6. There is $2 left.	We change the $2 to 20 dimes and add the other 2 dimes. There are 22 dimes.	When we split 22 dimes 3 ways, each person gets 7 dimes. There is 1 dime left.	We change the dime to 10 cents and add the other 5 cents. Now we split 15 cents 3 ways.

```
      6              6.             6.7            6.75
  3)20.25        3)20.25       3)20.25        3)20.25
   -18            -18            -18            -18
    2              2.2            2.2            2.2
                                -2.1           -2.1
                                  .1            .15
                                              -.15
```

Solve.

```
        5.96             6.52            52.7            19.73
1. 8)47.68       2. 9)58.68      3. 6)316.2      4. 5)98.65
   -40              54             -30              -5
    76             -54             16               48
   -72              46            -12              -45
    48             -45             42               36
   -48              18            -42              -35
     0             -18              0               15
                     0                             -15
                                                     0
```

Write an equation. Then solve.

5. Imelda has 8.169 meters of rope. She wants to cut it into
3 equal pieces to make jump ropes for her 3 friends. How
long will each jump rope be?

```
     2.723
  3)8.169
   -6
    21
   -21
     06
    -6
     09
    -9
```

_____

6. Tonio has 7.47 pounds of rabbit food. He will divide it
equally among his 9 rabbits. How much food will each
rabbit get?

```
    0.83
  9)7.47
   -72
    27
   -27
```

_____

Class Activity

Name _____ Date _____

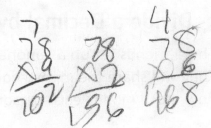

▶ Divide a Decimal by a Two-Digit Number

A company bought 38 sandwiches for a business meeting. Each sandwich costs the same amount. The sandwiches cost $161.12 in all. What was the price of each sandwich?

To answer this question, we have to divide the total price among the 38 sandwiches. We round the divisor, 38, up to 40 to estimate the multipliers.

When $161 is divided into 38 parts, each part is $4. There is $9 left.	We change the $9 to 90 dimes and add the other dime. There are 91 dimes.	When we split 91 dimes into 38 parts, each part is 2 dimes. There are 15 dimes left.	We change the 15 dimes to 150 pennies and add the other 2 pennies. Now we split 152 pennies 38 ways.

```
       4              4            4.2           4.24
(40) 38)161.12   (40) 38)161.12  (40) 38)161.12  (40) 38)161.12
     -152            -152            -152           -152
        9              9.1            9.1            9.1
                                    -7.6           -7.6
                                     1.5            1.52
                                                  -1.52
```

Solve.

7. 51)374.85

8. 22)580.8

9. 78)706.68

10. 36)547.2

Write an equation. Then solve.

11. A rectangle has an area of 35.75 square meters and a length of 11 meters. What is its width?

_____

12. Katsu bought 18 pounds of apples for $23.04. What was the price for each pound?

_____

11 m | Area = 33.75 sq. m

Divide Decimal Numbers by Whole Numbers

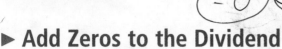

► Add Zeros to the Dividend

Adding zeros at the end of a number, *after* the decimal point, does not change the value of the number. This idea can help us solve some division problems.

Eight friends bought movie tickets. The total cost for the tickets was $78. How much did each friend pay?

When the $78 is divided among 8 people, each person pays $9, and there is $6 still left to divide.	Add a decimal point and a 0. Bring down the 0 (trade $6 for 60 dimes) and continue to divide. Each person pays 7 dimes more, and there are 4 dimes left to divide.	Add another 0 after the decimal point. Bring down the 0 (trade 4 dimes for 40 pennies) and finish dividing. Each person pays 5 pennies more, for a total of $9.75.

$$\begin{array}{r} 9 \\ 8\overline{)78} \\ -72 \\ \hline 6 \end{array} \qquad \begin{array}{r} 9.7 \\ 8\overline{)78.0} \\ -72 \\ \hline 6.0 \\ -5.6 \\ \hline .4 \end{array} \qquad \begin{array}{r} 9.75 \\ 8\overline{)78.00} \\ -72 \\ \hline 6.0 \\ -5.6 \\ \hline .40 \\ -.40 \end{array}$$

13. Jun rode her bike to the bookstore and back. According to her bike's odometer, the round trip distance was 6.65 miles. She started the division at the right to figure out the one-way distance to the bookstore. Add a 0 to the end of the dividend and finish the division.

The distance to the bookstore is ___3.325___ miles.

$$\begin{array}{r} 3.325 \\ 2\overline{)6.650} \\ -6 \\ \hline 0.6 \\ -.6 \\ \hline .05 \\ -.04 \\ \hline .010 \\ -.010 \\ \hline 0 \end{array}$$

Solve.

14. $6\overline{)54.75}$

15. $5\overline{)141.2}$

16. $8\overline{)310}$

17. $26\overline{)422.5}$

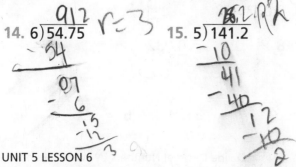

▶ Patterns in Division by Powers of 10

Recall that powers of 10, such as 10^1, 10^2, and 10^3 represent repeated multiplication with 10. The exponent tells you how many times to use 10 as a factor.

$10^1 = 10$ $10^2 = 10 \times 10 = 100$ $10^3 = 10 \times 10 \times 10 = 1,000$

Study the patterns in Exercises 18 and 19. Then complete Exercises 20–23.

18. $35.6 \div 10 = \underline{3.56}$

    $35.6 \div 100 = \underline{0.356}$

    $35.6 \div 1,000 = \underline{0.0356}$

19. $125 \div 10^1 = \underline{12.5}$

    $125 \div 10^2 = \underline{1.25}$

    $125 \div 10^3 = \underline{0.125}$

20. $50.7 \div 10^1 = \underline{5.07}$

    $50.7 \div 10^2 = \underline{0.507}$

    $50.7 \div 10^3 = \underline{0.057}$ 0.0507

21. $916.2 \div 10 = \underline{91.62}$

    $916.2 \div 100 = \underline{9.162}$

    $916.2 \div 1,000 = \underline{0.9162}$

22. $4,076 \div 10^1 = \underline{407.6}$

    $4,076 \div 10^2 = \underline{40.76}$

    $4,076 \div 10^3 = \underline{4.076}$

23. $7.8 \div 10^1 = \underline{0.78}$

    $7.8 \div 10^2 = \underline{0.078}$

    $7.8 \div 10^3 = \underline{0.0078}$

24. Complete these statements to summarize your work in Exercises 18–23.

    a. Dividing a number by 10^1, or 10, shifts the digits to the right _____1_____ place(s).

    b. Dividing a number by 10^2, or 100, shifts the digits to the right _____2_____ place(s).

    c. Dividing a number by 10^3, or 1,000, shifts the digits to the right _____3_____ place(s).

▶ Patterns Relating Multiplication and Division

Use the multiplication problem to help you solve the division problem.

25. $32 \div 8 = \underline{4}$

    $8 \times \underline{4} = 32$

27. $0.32 \div 8 = \underline{0.04}$

    $8 \times \underline{0.04} = 0.32$

26. $3.2 \div 8 = \underline{0.4}$

    $8 \times \underline{0.4} = 3.2$

28. $0.032 \div 8 = \underline{0.004}$

    $8 \times \underline{0.004} = 0.032$

Solve by using mental math.

29. $6.3 \div 9 = \underline{0.7}$

30. $0.15 \div 3 = \underline{0.05}$

31. $4.8 \div 6 = \underline{0.8}$

Divide Decimal Numbers by Whole Numbers

Name

Date

CA CC Content Standards **5.NBT.2, 5.NBT.7**
Mathematical Practices **MP.1, MP.2, MP.3, MP.6, MP.8**

► Use Money to See Shift Patterns

Jordan earns $243 a week. The money is shown here.

Jordan's Earnings in Dollars

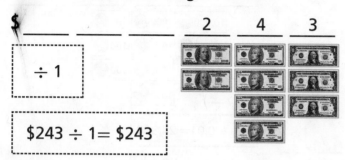

$ ____ ____ ____   2   4   3

÷ 1

$243 ÷ 1 = $243

Answer each question about how much Jordan earns in coins.

1. How many dimes ($0.10) does he earn?

2,430 dimes

Jordan's Earnings in Dimes

2 , 4 3 0

1000	100	10	
1000	100	10	
	100	10	
	100		

÷ 0.1

243 ÷ 0.1 = 2,430

2. What happens to each dollar? Why?

It becomes 10 dime as much
10 dimes in one dollar

3. What happens to the number showing Jordan's earnings? Why?

It becomes 10 as much
Each dollar becomes 10 dimes

4. When you divide by 0.1, does each digit shift right or left? Why?

left

5. How many places does each digit shift? Why?

1   10 times as great

► Use Money to See Shift Patterns (continued)

6. How many pennies ($0.01) does he earn?

24,300 Pennies

Jordan's Earnings in Pennies

	2	4	,	3	0	0

10,000 1000 100
10,000 1000 100
1000 100
1000

÷ 0.01

243 ÷ 0.01 = 24,300

7. What happens to each dollar?

They became $\frac{1}{100}$ as much

8. What happens to the number showing Jordan's earnings?

.9

It becomes 100 as much

9. When you divide by 0.01, does each digit shift right or left? Why?

left   dividing by 0.01 is the same as multiplying by 100

10. How many places does each digit shift? Why?

2   they represent 100 times as much

11. How many tenths of a cent ($0.001) does he earn?

243,000

Jordan's Earnings in Tenths of a Cent

	2	4	3	,	0	0	0

100,000 10,000 1000
100,000 10,000 1000   ÷ 0.001
10,000 1000
10,000   243 ÷ 0.001 = 243,000

12. What happens to each dollar?

They become $\frac{1}{1000}$ as much

13. What happens to the number showing Jordan's earnings? Why?

They become $\frac{1}{1,000}$ as much

14. When you divide by 0.001, does each digit shift right or left? Why?

left

15. How many places does each digit shift? Why?

3

Divide Whole Numbers by Decimal Numbers

Name _____   **Date** _____

▶ Relate Decimal Division to Multiplication

Solve.   *Show your work.*

16. Mrs. Moreno made 1 liter of grape jelly. She will pour it into jars that each hold 0.1 liter. How many jars will she need?

    Think: How many tenths are there in 1 whole? __10__

    Complete the equation: $1 \div 0.1 = $ __10__.

    This answer is the same as $1 \times$ __10__.

17. Mr. Moreno made 2 liters of spaghetti sauce. He will pour it into jars that each hold 0.1 liter. How many jars will he need?

    Think: How many tenths are there in 1 whole? __10__

    How many tenths are there in 2 wholes? __20__

    Complete the equation: $2 \div 0.1 = $ __20__.

    This answer is the same as $2 \times$ __10__.

18. The Morenos made a kiloliter of fruit punch for a large party. They will pour it into punch bowls that each hold 0.01 kiloliter. How many bowls will they need?

    Think: How many hundredths are there in 1 whole? __100__

    Complete the equation: $1 \div 0.01 = $ __100__.

    This answer is the same as $1 \times$ __100__.

19. When we divide a number by a decimal number less than one, why is the quotient greater than the original number?

    _____

    _____

    _____

    _____

© Houghton Mifflin Harcourt Publishing Company

UNIT 5 LESSON 7   Divide Whole Numbers by Decimal Numbers **183**

5-7 Class Activity

▶ What's the Error?

Dear Math Students,

I was absent today. My friend told me we learned to divide by 0.1 and 0.01. She said that when you divide by 0.1, the digits shift one place, and when you divide by 0.01, they shift two places. Here are two problems from my homework.

45 ÷ 0.1 = 4.5   45 ÷ 0.01 = 0.45

Are my answers correct? If not, can you explain what I did wrong?

Your friend,
Puzzled Penguin

20. Write a response to the Puzzled Penguin.

_____

_____

_____

▶ Change Decimal Divisors to Whole Numbers

You can use the strategy below to change a division problem with a decimal divisor to an equivalent problem with a whole number divisor.

Discuss each step used to find 6 ÷ 0.2.

Step 1: Write 6 ÷ 0.2 as a fraction.

$$6 \div 0.2 = \frac{6}{0.2}$$

Step 2: Make an equivalent fraction with a whole number divisor by multiplying $\frac{6}{0.2}$ by 1 in the form of $\frac{10}{10}$. Now you can divide 60 by 2.

$$\frac{6}{0.2} \times 1 = \frac{6}{0.2} \times \frac{10}{10} = \frac{60}{2}$$

21. Why is the answer to 60 ÷ 2 the same as the answer to 6 ÷ 0.2?

_____

_____

▶ Change Decimal Divisors to Whole Numbers (continued)

You can use the strategy of multiplying both numbers by 10 even when a division problem is given in long division format.

Step 1: Put a decimal point after the whole number.

$$0.2\overline{)6.}$$

Step 2: Multiply both numbers by 10, which shifts the digits one place left. Show this by moving the decimal point one place right. Add zeros if necessary.

$$0.2\overline{)6.0.}$$

Step 3: Instead of drawing arrows, you can make little marks called carets (^) to show where you put the "new" decimal points. Now divide 60 by 2.

$$0.2_\wedge\overline{)6.0_\wedge}\quad\begin{array}{r}3\,0.\end{array}$$

22. Why does moving both decimal points the same number of places give us the same answer?

_____

_____

Answer each question to describe how to find 6 ÷ 0.02 and 6 ÷ 0.002.

23. Suppose you want to find 6 ÷ 0.02.

By what number can you multiply 0.02 to get a whole number? _____

Describe and show how to move the decimal points to solve 6 ÷ 0.02 by long division. $0.02\overline{)6.}$

_____

24. Suppose you want to find 6 ÷ 0.002.

By what number can you multiply 0.002 to get a whole number? _____

Describe and show how to move the decimal points to solve 6 ÷ 0.002. $0.002\overline{)6.}$

_____

Name _____ **Date** _____

► Practice Dividing by Decimals

Solve.

25. $0.5\overline{)45}$ 26. $0.07\overline{)56}$ 27. $0.8\overline{)496}$ 28. $0.65\overline{)910}$

29. $0.12\overline{)60}$ 30. $0.004\overline{)16}$ 31. $0.9\overline{)468}$ 32. $0.75\overline{)270}$

33. $0.3\overline{)96}$ 34. $0.06\overline{)42}$ 35. $0.072\overline{)216}$ 36. $2.4\overline{)192}$

Solve.   *Show your work.*

37. A dime weighs about 0.08 ounce. Jake has a pound
    (16 ounces) of dimes. About how many dimes does
    he have?

    _____

38. A quarter weighs about 0.2 ounce. Naoki has
    2 pounds (32 ounces) of quarters. About how
    many quarters does he have?

    _____

39. A dime is about 0.14 centimeter thick. Zeynep
    made a stack of dimes 35 centimeters high.
    About how many dimes did she use?

    _____

40. A newborn mouse weighs about 0.25 ounce. A
    newborn cat weighs about 4 ounces. A newborn cat
    weighs how many times as much as a newborn mouse?

    _____

Divide Whole Numbers by Decimal Numbers

Name

Date

CA CC Content Standards **5.NBT.2, 5.NBT.7**
Mathematical Practices **MP.1, MP.2, MP.3, MP.6, MP.7**

▶ Use Money to See Shift Patterns

It costs $0.312 (31 cents and $\frac{2}{10}$ cent) to make one Cat's Eye Marble. The money is shown here.

Cost of a Cat's Eye Marble

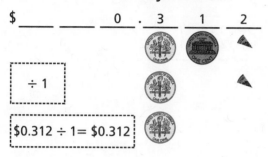

$ ___ ___ 0 . 3 1 2

÷ 1

$0.312 ÷ 1= $0.312

Answer each question about the different coins.

1. How many dimes ($0.10) does it cost to make one Cat's Eye Marble?

   3.12

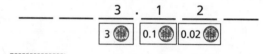

___ ___ 3 . 1 2

3 | 0.1 | 0.02

÷ 0.1

0.312 ÷ 0.1= 3.12

2. What happens to the number that shows the cost?

3. When you divide by 0.1, does each digit shift to the right or left? Why?

4. How many places does each digit shift? Why?

© Houghton Mifflin Harcourt Publishing Company

▶ Use Money to See Shift Patterns (continued)

5. How many pennies ($0.01) does it cost to make one Cat's Eye Marble?

_____

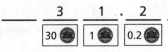

$\div 0.01$

$0.312 \div 0.01 = 31.2$

6. What happens to the number that shows the cost?

_____

7. When you divide by 0.01, does each digit shift to the right or left? Why?

_____

8. How many places does each digit shift? Why?

_____

9. How many tenths of a cent ($0.001) does it cost to make one Cat's Eye Marble?

_____

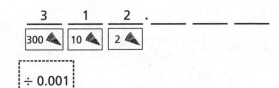

$\div 0.001$

10. What happens to the number that shows the cost?

_____

$0.312 \div 0.001 = 312$

11. When you divide by 0.001, does each digit shift to the right or left? How many places? Why?

_____

12. Are the shift patterns for dividing by 0.1, 0.01, and 0.001 the same when the product (dividend) is a decimal number as when the product (dividend) is a whole number? Why or why not?

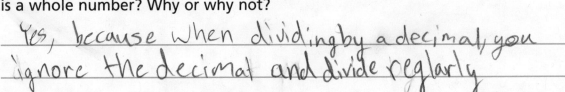

Yes, because when dividing by a decimal, you ignore the decimal and divide reglarly

© Houghton Mifflin Harcourt Publishing Company

Divide with Two Decimal Numbers

▶ Change Decimal Divisors to Whole Numbers

To divide a decimal by a decimal, use the same strategy
you used when you divided a whole number by a decimal.

Discuss each step used to find 0.06 ÷ 0.2.

Step 1: Write 0.06 ÷ 0.2 as a fraction.

$$0.06 \div 0.2 = \frac{0.06}{0.2}$$

Step 2: Make an equivalent fraction
with a whole number divisor by
multiplying $\frac{0.06}{0.2}$ by 1 in the form
of $\frac{10}{10}$. Now divide 0.6 by 2.

$$\frac{0.06}{0.2} \times 1 = \frac{0.06}{0.2} \times \frac{10}{10} = \frac{0.6}{2}$$

13. Why does 0.06 ÷ 0.2 have the same answer as 0.6 ÷ 2?

_____

_____

_____

**Here are the steps for using the strategy when the problem
is in long division form.**

Step 1: Set up the problem.

$$0.2\,\overline{)\,0.06}$$

Step 2: Multiply both numbers by 10. This shifts
the digits one place left. Show this by
moving the decimal point one place right.

$$0.2_\wedge\,\overline{)\,0.0_\wedge 6}$$

Step 3: You don't have to draw arrows. Carets (^)
show where each "new" decimal point
belongs. Now divide 0.6 by 2.

$$0.2_\wedge\,\overline{)\,0.0_\wedge 6}^{\,.3}$$

14. Why does moving both decimal points the
same number of places give a problem with
the same answer as the original problem?

_____

_____

_____

Name _____ **Date** _____

▶ Change Decimal Divisors to Whole Numbers (continued)

15. How would you solve 0.06 ÷ 0.02 with long division? What number do you need to multiply both numbers by to make 0.02 a whole number?

$$0.02\overline{)0.06}$$

_____

_____

_____

16. How would you solve 0.06 ÷ 0.002 with long division? What number do you need to multiply both numbers by to make 0.002 a whole number?

$$0.002\overline{)0.06}$$

_____

_____

Solve each division problem. Show your work.

17. $0.9\overline{)7.2}$ **18.** $0.04\overline{)0.364}$ **19.** $0.6\overline{)0.372}$ **20.** $0.14\overline{)7.28}$

Write an equation. Then solve.

21. A sand and gravel company has 12.6 tons of gravel to haul today. Each truck can carry 0.9 ton of gravel. How many trucks will be needed?

_____ *g* _____

22. A developer is building an amusement park on a rectangular lot with an area of 1.35 square miles. The length of one side of the lot is 0.45 mile. What is the length of the other side?

_____ *a* _____

0.45 mi | Area = 1.35 sq. mi | ?

Divide with Two Decimal Numbers

Name _____ **Date** _____

CA CC Content Standards **5.NBT.6, 5.NBT.7**
Mathematical Practices **MP.1, MP.2, MP.7**

▶ Divide Mentally

Use the fact that 1,715 ÷ 35 = 49 to solve each problem.

1. $35\overline{)17.15}$ *0.49*

2. $35\overline{)171.5}$ *4.9*

3. $0.35\overline{)17.15}$

4. $35\overline{)17,150}$

5. $3.5\overline{)1,715}$

6. $0.35\overline{)1,715}$

7. $3.5\overline{)17.15}$

8. $0.35\overline{)1,715}$

▶ Solve Division Problems

Solve. If both numbers are whole numbers, give your answer as a whole number with a remainder.

9. $0.6\overline{)54}$

10. $0.08\overline{)72}$

11. $0.5\overline{)0.45}$

12. $0.07\overline{)0.49}$

13. $0.05\overline{)34.5}$

14. $7\overline{)395}$ *96*

15. $0.045\overline{)41.85}$

16. $42\overline{)4,009}$

17. $0.02\overline{)98.8}$ *49*

18. $6\overline{)980}$

19. $0.04\overline{)117}$

20. $0.081\overline{)64.881}$

Name _____ **Date** _____

$$\begin{array}{r}28\\+28\\\hline 56\end{array}\qquad\begin{array}{r}56\\+28\\\hline 84\end{array}$$

▶ Check for Reasonable Answers

Solve. Check that your answer is reasonable.

Show your work.

21. The Clark family is having a big lawn party. They have 196 chairs, and they want to put 8 chairs at each table. How many chairs will be left over?

_____

22. Liam needs to buy 640 eggs for a soccer breakfast. If eggs come in cartons of 18, how many cartons should he buy?

_____

23. Jacob made $507 this year delivering newspapers. If he makes the same amount monthly, how much money did he make each month?

_____

24. Johna and Pedro made a rectangular banner to display at the school volleyball game. The area of the banner is 7 square meters, and its length is 4 meters. What is the width of the banner?

_____

25. Lakisha and Raj went to an electronics store. Lakisha bought a television for $358.40. This is 28 times as much as Raj spent on a new video game. How much did Raj's video game cost?

$$\begin{array}{r}12\\28\overline{)358.40}\\-28\\\hline 78\end{array}$$

224

_____

26. The Ramsey family collects and sells maple syrup. Last month they collected 57.8 liters of syrup. They will pour it into bottles that hold 0.85 liter. How many bottles will the Ramseys fill?

_____

27. Kyle spent $27.28 on postage stamps today. Each stamp cost 44 cents ($0.44). How many stamps did Kyle buy?

_____

Division Practice

Name _____   **Date** _____

CA CC Content Standards **5.NBT.5, 5.NBT.6, 5.NBT.7, 5.NF.5, 5.NF.5a** Mathematical Practices **MP.1, MP.2, MP.3, MP.6, MP.8**

▶ Multiply or Divide?

Read the problem. Then answer the questions.

1. A turtle walks 0.2 mile in 1 hour. How far can it walk in 0.5 hour?

   a. Do you need to multiply or divide to solve? ___multiply___

   b. Will the answer be more or less than 0.2 miles? _more_____

   c. What is the answer? _____

2. Gus ran 3.6 miles. He took a sip of water every 0.9 mile. How many sips did he take?

   a. Do you need to multiply or divide to solve? _____

   b. Will the answer be greater or less than 3.6? _____

   c. What is the answer? _____

3. Last year 135 cows on Dixie's Dairy Farm had calves. This year 0.6 times that many cows had calves. How many cows had calves this year?

   a. Do you need to multiply or divide to solve? _____

   b. Will the answer be greater or less than 135? _____

   c. What is the answer? _____

4. A box contains 1.2 pounds of cereal. A serving weighs 0.08 pounds. How many servings are in the box?

   a. Do you need to multiply or divide to solve? _____

   b. Will the answer be greater or less than 1.2? _____

   c. What is the answer? _____

5. A rectangular patio has an area of 131.52 square meters. The width of the patio is 9.6 meters. What is its length?

   a. Do you need to multiply or divide to solve? _____

   b. Will the answer be greater or less than 131.52 meters? _____

   c. What is the answer? _____

▶ Results of Whole Number and Decimal Operations

Answer each question.

6. If a and b are whole numbers greater than 1, will $b \times a$ be greater than or less than a? Why?

_____

_____

7. If a is a whole number and d is a decimal less than 1, will $d \times a$ be greater than or less than a? Why?

_____

_____

8. If a and b are whole numbers greater than 1, will $a \div b$ be greater than or less than a? Why?

_____

_____

9. If a is a whole number and d is a decimal less than 1, will $a \div d$ be greater than or less than a? Why?

_____

_____

Use reasoning to compare the expressions. Write >, <, or =.
Do not compute the actual values.

10. $42 \times 356 \bigcirc 356 \div 42$

11. $0.65 \times 561 \bigcirc 561 \div 0.65$

12. $832 \div 67 \bigcirc 832 \div 0.67$

13. $738 \times 66 \bigcirc 738 \times 0.66$

14. $126 \div 0.9 \bigcirc 126 \times 0.9$

15. $3{,}500 \times 0.7 \bigcirc 3{,}500 \times 7$

16. $64 \times 0.64 \bigcirc 64 \div 0.64$

17. $5{,}602 \div 42 \bigcirc 5{,}602 \div 0.42$

Distinguish Between Multiplication and Division

▶ Make Predictions

Solve.

Show your work.

18. Farmer Ortigoza has 124.6 acres of land. Farmer Ruben has 0.8 times as much land as Farmer Ortigoza.

   a. Does Farmer Ruben have more or less than 124.6 acres?

   _____

   b. How many acres does Farmer Ruben have? _____

19. Mee Young has 48 meters of crepe paper. She will cut it into strips that are each 0.6 meter long.

   a. Will Mee Young get more or fewer than 48 strips?

   _____

   b. How many strips will Mee Young get? _80 strips_____

20. Jenn's garden is a rectangle with length 3.5 meters and width 0.75 meters.

   a. Is the area of the garden greater or less than 3.5 square meters?

   _____

   b. What is the area of the garden? _____

21. Roberto can lift 103.5 pounds. That is 0.9 times the amount his friend Vance can lift.

   a. Can Vance lift more or less than 103.5 pounds?

   _____

   b. How many pounds can Vance lift? _____

22. The Daisy Cafe served 18 liters of hot chocolate today. Each serving was in a cup that held 0.2 liter.

   a. Did the cafe serve more or fewer than 18 cups of hot chocolate?

   _____

   b. How many cups did the cafe serve? _____

▶ Mixed Practice

Solve. Check your work.

23. $6\overline{)5.1}$

24. $4\overline{)22.8}$

25. $27\overline{)8.91}$

26. $34\overline{)1.564}$

27. $\begin{array}{r} 0.4 \\ \times\ 0.8 \\ \hline \end{array}$

28. $\begin{array}{r} 28 \\ \times\ 0.63 \\ \hline \end{array}$

29. $\begin{array}{r} 0.35 \\ \times\ 94 \\ \hline \end{array}$

30. $\begin{array}{r} 78.6 \\ \times\ 49 \\ \hline \end{array}$

31. $0.8\overline{)7.52}$

32. $0.13\overline{)689}$

33. $0.96\overline{)460.8}$

34. $1.9\overline{)1.634}$

35. $\begin{array}{r} 0.37 \\ \times\ 0.09 \\ \hline \end{array}$

36. $\begin{array}{r} 0.75 \\ \times\ 0.14 \\ \hline \end{array}$

37. $\begin{array}{r} 51.3 \\ \times\ 6.2 \\ \hline \end{array}$

38. $\begin{array}{r} 4.29 \\ \times\ 0.27 \\ \hline \end{array}$

▶ Mixed Real World Applications

Solve. Check that your answer is reasonable.

Show your work.

39. Polly bought 12 beach balls for her beach party. She spent $23.64. How much did each beach ball cost?

_____

40. The 245 fifth graders at Miller School are going on a trip to the aquarium. Each van can carry 16 students. How many vans will be needed for the trip?

_____

41. Today Aaliyah ran 4.5 miles per hour for three fourths (0.75) of an hour. How far did Aaliyah run today?

_____

Distinguish Between Multiplication and Division

Name _____

Date _____

CA CC Content Standards **5.NBT.7**
Mathematical Practices **MP.1, MP.7**

▶ Math and Currency

When you travel from one country to another, you sometimes need to exchange your currency for the currency used in the country you are visiting. An exchange rate is the rate at which one currency can be exchanged for another.

Currencies are usually compared to 1 U.S. dollar (1 USD) when they are exchanged. For example, 1 USD may be exchanged for 6.5 Chinese yuans or 0.95 Canadian dollars. The exact amount of the exchange often varies from day to day.

Solve.

Show your work.

1. Suppose 5 U.S. dollars (5 USD) can be exchanged for 64 Mexican pesos. What operation would be used to find the value of 1 USD in pesos?

_____

Find the value of 1 USD in pesos. 1 USD = _____ pesos

► Math and Currency (continued)

Complete the exchange rate column of the table.

Country	Currency Unit		Equivalent Amounts	Exchange Rate
2. Japan	yen		20 USD = 1,530 yen	1 USD = _____ yen
3. England	pound		10 USD = 6.1 pounds	1 USD = _____ pounds
4. Germany	Euro		50 USD = 35 Euros	1 USD = _____ Euros

Visiting another country often means exchanging more than 1 USD for the currency of that country.

5. The exchange rate for francs, the currency of Switzerland, is 10 USD = 8.8 francs. At that rate, how many francs would be exchanged for 25 USD?

_____

6. A traveler in Latvia exchanged 5 USD for 2.6 lats. At that rate, what is the cost of a souvenir in lats if the cost is 3 USD?

_____

7. A tourist would like to exchange 100 USD for kuna, the currency of Croatia. At the rate 12 USD = 66 kuna, how many kuna should the tourist receive?

_____

8. The cost to visit a famous tourist attraction in Russia is 381.25 rubles. What is the cost in USD if the exchange rate is 3 USD = 91.5 rubles?

_____

Focus on Mathematical Practices

1. Select the expression that involves a shift of the digits to the right 2 places. Mark all that apply.

   Ⓐ $9 \div 1{,}000$

   Ⓑ $30 \div 10^2$

   Ⓒ $2 \div 10^3$

   Ⓓ $7 \div 10$

   Ⓔ $400 \div 10^1$

   Ⓕ $8 \div 100$

2. Classify each quotient as being equal to 52, equal to 5.2, or equal to 0.52. Write the letter of the quotient in the correct box.

   A $52 \div 10^2$ B $52 \div 10^1$ C $520 \div 10^1$

   D $520 \div 10^2$ E $520 \div 10^3$ F $5{,}200 \div 10^3$

52	5.2	0.52

3. Explain why $0.04\overline{)3.6}$ has the same answer as $4\overline{)360}$.

4. Why does dividing 5 by a decimal less than 1 give a quotient greater than 5?

5. A farmer ships 4 times as many oranges as tangerines. The farmer ships 8,260 oranges. How many tangerines does he ship? Write an equation. Then solve.

6. Jamal buys postcards of Washington, D.C., for $10.20, not including tax. Each postcard costs $0.85. How many postcards does Jamal buy?

_____ postcards

7. Paige's backyard has an area of 95.9 square meters. The length of the yard is 14 meters, what is its width?

14 m

Area = 95.9 m² ?

_____ meters

8. Mr. Adams divides 223 markers equally among the 26 students in his class. He puts the extra markers in a box. What is the least number of markers he puts in the box?

_____ markers

9. A park creates new habitats for 182 monkeys. Each habitat will house 8 or fewer monkeys.

Part A

What is the least number of habitats the zoo will need?

_____ habitats

Part B

What did you do with the remainder? Explain why.

10. Solve. Express the remainder as a whole number. Show your work. Draw a model to show how you solved the problem.

57)970

11. Circle the word or phrase that makes the sentence true.

When you divide by 100, each digit shifts

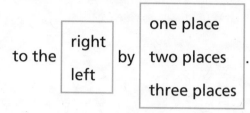

to the [right / left] by [one place / two places / three places] .

12. Select each quotient that is correct. Mark all that apply.

Ⓐ $300 \div 100 = 3$

Ⓑ $3 \div 10 = 0.03$

Ⓒ $27 \div 100 = 0.27$

Ⓓ $60 \div 10 = 600$

13. Fill in the table to complete the pattern of dividing by powers of ten.

$4.72 \div 0.1$	4.72×10	_____
$4.72 \div 0.01$	$4.72 \times$ _____	472
$4.72 \div$ _____	$4.72 \times 1{,}000$	_____

14. Solve. $2{,}412 \div 3$. Explain how you know your answer is reasonable.

15. Nina is putting equal amounts of oatmeal into 4 containers. She has 37.6 ounces of oatmeal. How many ounces of oatmeal should she put into each container?

_____ ounces

16. Select each quotient equal to 0.28. Mark all that apply.

   (A) $2.8 \div 10^2$

   (B) $28 \div 10^3$

   (C) $280 \div 10^3$

   (D) $2.8 \div 10^1$

   (E) $28 \div 10^1$

17. Lunch for the band costs $137.20. The band has 56 members. How much does each member's lunch cost?

   $ _____

18. Marco got a quotient of 70 when he divided 49 by 0.07.

   Part A

   What is the correct answer for this problem?

   Part B

   What mistake did Marco make?

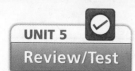

19. Write the letter of the expression next to the number that shows its quotient.

A 845 ÷ 27   ☐ 31 R4

B 190 ÷ 6   ☐ 24 R10

C 612 ÷ 15   ☐ 31 R8

D 363 ÷ 9   ☐ 24 R9

E 298 ÷ 12   ☐ 40 R12

F 441 ÷ 18   ☐ 40 R3

20. James lives 3.42 kilometers from school. Megan lives 0.76 kilometer from school. The distance James lives from school is how many times as long as the distance Megan lives from school? Show your work.

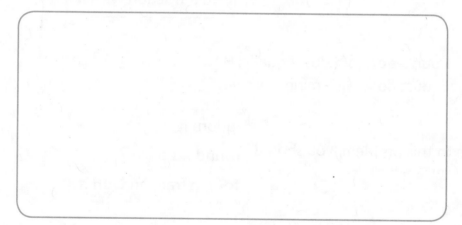

21. Fill in the table to complete the pattern of dividing by powers of ten.

36 ÷ 10^1	36 ÷ 10	_____
36 ÷ 10^2	36 ÷ _____	0.36
36 ÷ 10–	36 ÷ 1000	_____

For numbers 22a–22c, read the word problem and circle the phrase from the box that make the sentence correct.

22a. In a movie, 289 aliens plan to visit Earth. Each ship can hold as many as 3 aliens. What is the least number of ships needed?

For the remainder in this problem, you should

> ignore it
>
> round it up
>
> form a fraction with it

22b. Basma cuts ribbon to tie onto balloons for the carnival. She has 925.6 inches of ribbon in all. If each ribbon must be 24 inches long, how many ribbons can she cut?

For the remainder in this problem, you should

> ignore it
>
> round it up
>
> form a fraction with it

22c. Six miners divide 15 ounces of gold dust equally. How many ounces of gold dust does each miner receive?

For the remainder in this problem, you should

> ignore it
>
> round it up
>
> form a fraction with it

23. Write the correct number in each box in the place value sections to find the quotient.

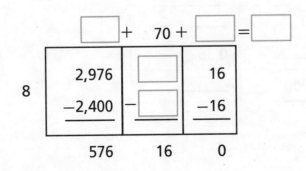

Family Letter

Content Overview

Dear Family,

In Unit 6 of *Math Expressions*, your child will apply the skills they have learned about operations with fractions, whole numbers, and decimals as they solve real world problems involving addition, subtraction, multiplication, and division.

A *situation equation* shows the structure of the information in a problem. A *solution equation* shows the operation that can be used to solve a problem. Your child will review situation and solution equations for addition and subtraction, and for multiplication and division. These methods of representing problems are particularly helpful when problems involve larger numbers that students cannot add, subtract, multiply, or divide mentally.

Your child will also solve multiplication and addition comparison problems and compare those types of problems, identifying how they are the same and how they are different.

Addition Comparison Problem	**Multiplication Comparison Problem**
Terrell has 144 soccer trading cards. Manuel has 3 more cards than Terrell. How many cards does Manuel have?	Elena has 74 stamps in her collection. Hassan has 3 times as many stamps. How many stamps does Hassan have?

Students learn that in the addition problem, they are adding 3, and multiplying by 3 in the multiplication problem.

Solving multistep problems is an important Grade 5 skill. Your child begins by solving one-step problems, then moves to two-step problems, and finally solves multistep problems which involve more than two steps. Your child will represent and use visual models and equations to find solutions for these problems.

Sincerely,
Your child's teacher

© Houghton Mifflin Harcourt Publishing Company

 CA CC

This unit addresses the following standards from the *Common Core State Standards for Mathematics with California Additions*: 5.OA.1, 5.NBT.4, 5.NBT.5, 5.NBT.6, 5.NBT.7, 5.NF.1, 5.NF.2, 5.NF.3, 5.NF.4, 5.NF.4a, 5.NF.4b, 5.NF.5, 5.NF.5a, 5.NF.5b, 5.NF.6, 5.NF.7, 5.NF.7a, 5.NF.7b, 5.NF.7c, and all Mathematical Practices.

Estimada familia,

En la Unidad 6 de *Math Expressions*, su niño aplicará las destrezas que ha aprendido acerca de operaciones con fracciones, y números enteros y decimales, para resolver problemas de la vida cotidiana que involucren suma, resta, multiplicación y división.

Una *ecuación de situación* muestra la estructura de la información en un problema. Una *ecuación de solución* muestra la operación que se puede usar para resolver el problema. Su niño repasará ecuaciones de situación y de solución para suma y resta, y para multiplicación y división. Estos métodos de representar problemas son particularmente útiles cuando los problemas involucran números grandes que los estudiantes no pueden sumar, restar, multiplicar ni dividir mentalmente.

Su niño también resolverá problemas de comparación con multiplicación y con suma, y comparará ese tipo de problemas, identificando sus diferencias y semejanzas.

Problema de comparación con suma	**Problema de comparación con multiplicación**
Terrell tiene 144 tarjetas coleccionables de fútbol. Manuel tiene 3 tarjetas más. ¿Cuántas tarjetas tiene Manuel?	Elena tiene 74 estampillas en su colección. Hassan tiene el triple de estampillas. ¿Cuántas estampillas tiene Hassan?

Los estudiantes deben notar que en el problema con suma, suman 3 y en el problema con multiplicación multiplican por 3.

Resolver problemas de varios pasos es una destreza importante del 5.° grado. Su niño comenzará resolviendo problemas de un paso, luego de dos y finalmente resolverá problemas de varios pasos que tengan más de dos pasos. Usará modelos visuales y ecuaciones para representar y solucionar esos problemas.

Atentamente,
El maestro su niño

CA CC

Esta unidad se aplican los siguientes estándares auxiliares, contenidos en los *Estándares estatales comunes de matemáticas con adiciones para California*: 5.OA.1, 5.NBT.4, 5.NBT.5, 5.NBT.6, 5.NBT.7, 5.NF.1, 5.NF.2, 5.NF.3, 5.NF.4, 5.NF.4a, 5.NF.4b, 5.NF.5, 5.NF.5a, 5.NF.5b, 5.NF.6, 5.NF.7, 5.NF.7a, 5.NF.7b, 5.NF.7c, y todos los de prácticas matemáticas.

Name _____ **Date** _____

CA CC Content Standards **5.NBT.7, 5.NF.2**
Mathematical Practices **MP.1, MP.2, MP.4, MP.6**

> **VOCABULARY**
> situation equation
> solution equation

► Write Equations to Solve Problems

A **situation equation** shows the structure of the information in a problem. A **solution equation** shows the operation that can be used to solve a problem.

Read the problem and answer the questions.

1. Last night, 312 people attended the early showing of a theater movie. How many people attended the late showing if the total attendance for both showings was 961 people?

   a. The number of people who attended the first showing is known. Write the number.

   _312_

   b. Write a situation equation to represent the problem. Use the letter n to represent the unknown number of people.

   _$961 - 312 = n$_

   c. Write a solution equation to solve the problem.

   _$n = 961 - 312$_

   d. Solve your equation.

   $n = 649$ people

   Show your work.

Write an equation to solve the problem. Draw a model if you need to.

2. A shopper spent $53.50 for a sweater and a T-shirt. What was the cost of the sweater if the cost of the T-shirt was $16.50?

   _$53.50 - 16.50 = j$, $j = 37_

3. Jalen had $4\frac{2}{3}$ pounds of modeling clay and used $3\frac{1}{2}$ pounds for a craft project. How many pounds of clay were not used?

   $4\frac{2}{3} - 3\frac{1}{2} = 1\frac{1}{6}$ pounds

   $4\frac{2}{3} \times 4 = 16\frac{8}{12}$
   $3\frac{1}{2} \times 7 = 21$

4. Deborah drove 105.9 miles after stopping to rest. How many miles did she drive before the stop if she drove 231.7 miles altogether?

   126.8 miles

   231.7
   $- 105.9$
   125.8

Name _____ Date _____

handwritten top margin:
$$6,437.5$$
$$-422.3$$
$$\overline{6,015.2}$$

$$15\tfrac{1}{8}$$
$$-12\tfrac{1}{4}$$

▶ Practice

Write an equation and use it to solve the problem.
Draw a model if you need to.

5. A car odometer showed 6,437.5 miles at the end of a trip. How many miles did the odometer show at the beginning of the trip if the car was driven 422.3 miles?

   handwritten: $6,437.5 - 422.3 = 6,015.2$ miles

6. Enrique has two packages to mail. The weight of one package is $12\tfrac{1}{4}$ pounds. What is the weight of the second package if the total weight of the packages is $15\tfrac{1}{8}$ pounds?

   handwritten: $12\tfrac{1}{4} - 15\tfrac{1}{8} = 2\tfrac{7}{8}$ pounds

7. At a track and field meet, Cody's time in a sprint event was 17.6 seconds. What was Shaina's time if she completed the event in 1.08 fewer seconds?

   handwritten right margin: 17.6 $-\;1.08$

   handwritten: 16.52 seconds

▶ Reasonable Answers

Use your reasoning skills to complete Problems 8 and 9.

8. Suppose you were asked to add the decimals at the right, and you wrote 2.07 as your answer. Without using pencil and paper to actually add the decimals, give a reason why an answer of 2.07 is not reasonable.

   $$2.65$$
   $$+\,0.42$$

   _____

9. Suppose you were asked to subtract the fractions at the right, and you wrote $\tfrac{5}{6}$ as your answer. Without using pencil and paper to actually subtract the fractions, give a reason why an answer of $\tfrac{5}{6}$ is not reasonable.

   $$\tfrac{1}{2} - \tfrac{1}{3}$$

   handwritten: When you subtract fractions yo

Situation and Solution Equations for Addition and Subtraction

CA CC Content Standards 5.NBT.5, 5.NBT.6, 5.NBT.7, 5.NF4, 5.NF.4b, 5.NF.6, 5.NF.7, 5.NF.7c
Mathematical Practices MP.1, MP.2, MP.4, MP.6, MP.7

25

▶ Write Equations to Solve Problems

Sometimes it is helpful to write a situation equation and a solution equation to solve a problem. Other times you may write only a solution equation.

Read the problem and answer the questions.

1. On the first day of soccer practice, $\frac{2}{5}$ of the players were wearing new shoes. The team has 20 players. How many players were wearing new shoes?

   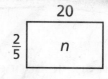

   a. The number of players wearing new shoes is given as a fraction. Write the fraction.

   $\frac{2}{5}$

   b. The number of players on the whole team is given. Write the number.

   20

   c. You are being asked to find a fraction of a whole. Write a solution equation to represent this fact.

   $20 \times \frac{2}{5} = n$

   d. Solve your equation.

   $n = 8$ players

Write an equation to solve the problem. Draw a model if you need to.

Show your work.

2. The musicians in a marching band are arranged in equal rows, with 8 musicians in each row. Altogether, the band has 104 musicians. In how many rows are the musicians marching?

   $104 \div 8 = g, \quad g = 12$ rows

3. Elena has chosen carpet that costs $4.55 per square foot for a rectangular floor that measures $12\frac{1}{2}$ feet by $14\frac{1}{2}$ feet. How many square feet of carpet is needed to cover the floor?

   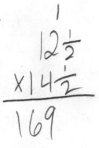

   $12\frac{1}{2} \times 14\frac{1}{2} = f, \quad f = 181\frac{1}{4}$ sq. ft

▶ Practice

Write an equation and use it to solve the problem.
Draw a model if you need to.

4. How many individual pieces of cheese, each weighing $\frac{1}{4}$ lb, can be cut from a block of cheese weighing 5 pounds?

_____

5. An online business receives an average of 140 orders per hour. At that rate, how many orders would the business expect to receive in 24 hours?

_____

6. A supermarket owner's cost for a 26-ounce can of coffee is $6.75. A case of coffee contains 12 cans. What profit is earned for each case sold if each can sells for $9.49?

_____

▶ Reasonable Answers

Use your reasoning skills to complete Problems 7 and 8.

7. Suppose you were asked to multiply the numbers at the right, and you wrote 15,000 as your answer. Without using pencil and paper to actually multiply the numbers, give a reason why an answer of 15,000 is not reasonable.

$2,500 \times 0.6$

_____

_____

8. Suppose you were asked to divide the numbers at the right, and you wrote 30 as your answer. Without using pencil and paper to actually divide the numbers, give a reason why an answer of 30 is not reasonable.

$90 \div \frac{1}{3}$

_____

_____

Situation and Solution Equations for Multiplication and Division

CA CC Content Standards **5.NF.4a, 5.NF.7a, 5.NF.7b**
Mathematical Practices **MP.1, MP.2, MP.4, MP.6**

▶ Write Multiplication Word Problems

Write a word problem for the equation.
Draw a model to show the product.

Show your work.

1. $\frac{3}{4} \cdot 2 = \frac{6}{4}$

_____

_____

_____

_____

_____

2. $\frac{5}{6} \cdot \frac{1}{3} = \frac{5}{18}$

_____

_____

_____

_____

_____

3. $\$6 \cdot 3.5 = \$21$

_____

_____

_____

_____

_____

Name _____   Date _____

Show your work.

▶ Write Division Word Problems

Write a word problem for the equation.
Draw a model to show the quotient.

4. $\frac{1}{4} \div 2 = \frac{1}{8}$

_____

_____

_____

_____

_____

5. $3 \div \frac{1}{2} = 6$

_____

_____

_____

_____

_____

_____

6. $\$16.50 \div 3 = \$5.50$

_____

_____

_____

_____

_____

_____

Name

Date

CA CC Content Standards **5.NBT.4, 5.NBT.6, 5.NBT.7, 5.NF.1, 5.NF.2**
Mathematical Practices **MP.1, MP.2, MP.4, MP.6**

▶ Use Rounding to Determine Reasonableness

Write an equation and use it to solve the problem.
Use rounding to show that your answer is reasonable.

Show your work.

1. Altogether, 91,292 people live in Waterloo and Muscatine, two cities in Iowa. The population of Waterloo is 68,406 people. What is the population of Muscatine?

   Equation and answer: $91,292 - 68,406 = j,$ $j = 22,886$

   Estimate: $23,000 = 91,000 - 68,000$

2. Vernon spent $229.06 for groceries, and paid for his purchase with five $50 bills. What amount of change should he have received?

   Equation and answer: 20.94

   Estimate: 229

▶ Use Estimation and Mental Math to Determine Reasonableness

Write an equation to solve the problem. Use estimation and mental math to show that your answer is reasonable.

3. In a school gymnasium, 588 students were seated for an assembly in 21 equal rows. What number of students were seated in each row?

   Equation and answer: $588 \div 21 = k,$ $k = 28$ rows

   Estimate: $600 \div 20 = f,$ $f =$

4. To get ready for her first semester of school, Jayna spent a total of $7.92 for eight identical notebooks. What was the cost of each notebook?

   Equation and answer: $7.92 \div 8 = h,$ $h,$ $h = 0.99$

   Estimate: $\$8.00 \div 8 = \$1.00$

$$\frac{5}{8} + \frac{15}{16} = \frac{10}{16} + \frac{15}{16} = \frac{25}{16} = 1\frac{9}{16}$$

► Use Benchmark Fractions to Determine Reasonableness

Write an equation and use it to solve the problem. Use benchmark fractions to verify that your answer is reasonable.

5. A $\frac{5}{8}$-inch thick paperback book is placed on top of a $\frac{15}{16}$-inch thick paperback book. What is the total thickness of books?

   Equation and answer: $\frac{5}{8} + \frac{15}{16} = k,$ $k = 1\frac{9}{16}$ inches

   Estimate: _____

   _____

6. A cabinetmaker cut $\frac{7}{16}$ inch off a board that was $2\frac{7}{8}$ inches long. What is the new length of the board?

   Equation and answer: _____

   Estimate: _____

   _____

► Predict to Check for Reasonableness

Write an equation and use it to solve the problem. Use mental math to identify two whole numbers your answer should be between.

7. A $45 award will be shared equally by 6 friends. In dollars, what is each friend's share of the award?

   Equation and answer: _____

   Estimate: _____

   _____

8. Four runners competed in a 10-kilometer relay race. Each runner ran the same distance. What was that distance?

   Equation and answer: _____

   Estimate: _____

   _____

Reasonable Answers

Name _____ **Date** _____

CA CC Content Standards **5.NBT.5**
Mathematical Practices **MP.1, MP.2, MP.4**

VOCABULARY
comparison

► The Jump Rope Contest

In **comparison** problems, you compare two amounts by addition or by multiplication. Draw comparison bars when needed.

Solve.

Show your work.

1. Julia jumped 1,200 times. Samantha jumped 1,100 times. How many more jumps did Julia do?

   100 more jumps

2. Ahanu jumped 1,050 times. Rolando jumped 1,080 times. How many fewer jumps did Ahanu do than Rolando?

   30 times fewer

3. Altogether the Blue Team jumped 11,485 times. The Red Team did 827 more jumps than the Blue Team. How many jumps did the Red Team do?

   12,312 jumps

   $$\begin{array}{r} 11,485 \\ +\quad 827 \\ \hline 12,312 \end{array}$$

4. Altogether the Green Team jumped 10,264 times. The Yellow Team did 759 fewer jumps than the Green Team. How many jumps did the Yellow Team do?

   9,505 jumps

   $$\begin{array}{r} 10,264 \\ -\quad 759 \\ \hline \end{array}$$

5. Ted jumped 1,300 times. He did 100 more jumps than Mario. How many jumps did Mario do?

   1200 jumps

   $$\begin{array}{r} 1300 \\ - \end{array}$$

6. Isaac jumped 987 times. Carlos needs to do 195 more jumps to tie with Isaac. How many jumps has Carlos done so far?

   792 jumps

   $$\begin{array}{r} 987 \\ -195 \\ \hline 792 \end{array}$$

7. Altogether the fourth graders jumped 345,127 times. If the fifth graders had done 2,905 fewer jumps, there would have been a tie. How many jumps did the fifth graders do?

   348,032 jumps

   $$\begin{array}{r} 345,127 \\ +\quad 2,905 \\ \hline 348,032 \end{array}$$

► Comparison Problems

Solve each comparison problem.

Show your work.

8. Maria scored 6 points in the basketball game. Suzanne scored 4 times as many points as Maria. How many points did Suzanne score?

   24 points

9. Ramon scored 10 points at the volleyball game. That was 5 times as many as David scored. How many points did David score? (Hint: Did David score more or fewer points than Ramon?)

   2 points

10. Ana has $15 in the bank. Her sister Benita has $\frac{1}{3}$ as much money in the bank. How much money does Benita have in the bank?

    $5

11. Dana has 9 CDs. She has $\frac{1}{5}$ as many as Sonya. How many CDs does Sonya have?

    45 CDs

12. Mr. Wagner has 32 horses on his farm. He has 4 times as many horses as Mr. Cruz. How many horses does Mr. Cruz have?

    8 horses

13. Chester has 49 CDs. Tony has $\frac{1}{7}$ as many as Chester. How many CDs does Tony have?

    7 CDs

14. A restaurant offers 18 types of pizza. A small cafe offers $\frac{1}{3}$ as many types of pizza. How many fewer types of pizza does the small cafe offer?

    6 pizzas

© Houghton Mifflin Harcourt Publishing Company

Language of Comparison Problems

CA CC Content Standards **5.NBT.5, 5.NBT.6, 5.NBT.7,
5.NF.5, 5.NF.5a, 5.NF.5b, 5.NF.6, 5.NF.7c** Mathematical
Practices **MP.1, MP.2, MP.3, MP.4, MP.6, MP.7, MP.8**

► Model and Solve Comparison Problems

The model below represents the time a student worked on spelling
(*s*) and math (*m*) homework. Use the model for Problems 1–3.

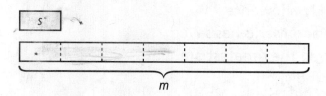

1. Write a comparison sentence that includes the words
   "as long as" and compares

   a. *m* to *s*. M is seven times as long as s

   b. *s* to *m*. S is one seventh as long as m

2. Write a comparison equation that compares

   a. *m* to *s*. $m = 7 \times s$ ($m = 7s$

   b. *s* to *m*. $s = \frac{1}{7} \times m$ ($s = \frac{1}{7}m$

3. Write a division equation that compares *s* to *m*.

   $s = m \div 7$

Solve. Draw a model if you need to.

4. The length of an unstretched spring is 120 cm. How long (*l*)
   will the spring be if it is stretched to 3 times that length?

   $120 \times 3 = 360$ cm

5. The length of a collapsed length fishing pole is *c*, which
   is $\frac{1}{8}$ times as long as its extended length. The extended
   length of the pole is 16 feet. What is its collapsed length?

   2 feet

6. A maple tree in the backyard of a home has a
   height of 0.75 meters. How many times as tall (*t*)
   is a nearby hickory tree that is 9 meters tall?

   12 times

6-6

Class Activity

Name _____   **Date** _____

▶ Multiplication and Scaling

You can predict how resizing one factor will affect a product.

Solve.

7. Gina and Mario each receive a weekly allowance.
   So far this year, Gina has saved $20 and Mario has saved
   0.4 times that amount. Who has saved the greatest amount
   of money? Multiply to check your prediction.

   Prediction: _Gina_____

8. Last week Camila worked 40 hours. Sergio worked $\frac{4}{5}$ that
   length of time. Which person worked more hours last week?

   Prediction: _Camila_____

9. On a math quiz, Juan was asked to find these two products:

   $$3 \times 10.6 \qquad 2.7 \times 10.6$$

   a. Without using pencil and paper to actually find
      the products, how will the product of 3×10.6 compare
      to the product of 2.7×10.6? Explain your answer.

      _____

   b. How will the product of 2.7×10.6 compare to the
      product of 3×10.6? Explain your answer.

      _____

   _31.8_
   _28.62_

10. Vanessa was asked this question on a math quiz:

    *How does the value of a fraction change when both
    the numerator and the denominator of the fraction
    are multiplied by the same number?*

    Explain how Vanessa should answer the question, and include
    an example to support your explanation.

    _____

    _____

    _____

    _____

    _____

    _____

© Houghton Mifflin Harcourt Publishing Company

CA CC Content Standards 5.NBT.5, 5.NBT.6, 5.NBT.7, 5.NF.2
Mathematical Practices MP.1, MP.2, MP.4, MP.6, MP.7

Name   Date

▶ Solve Comparison Problems

For each problem, draw a model and write *additive* or *multiplicative* to identify the type of comparison. Then write and solve an equation to solve the problem.

Show your model here.

1. Newborn baby Lila is 44.5 centimeters tall. Her older brother Tremaine is 4 times as tall. How tall (*t*) is Tremaine?

Type of comparison: multiplicative

Equation and answer: $44.5 \times 4 = t$, $t = 178$ centmeters

T [t   ]
L [44.5] (×4)

2. Brandon has $\frac{1}{4}$ cup of flour, and would like to make a recipe that requires $1\frac{5}{8}$ cups of flour. How many more cups (*c*) of flour are needed for the recipe?

Type of comparison: additive

Equation and answer: $1\frac{3}{8}$

Need [$1\frac{5}{8}$]
Has [$\frac{1}{4}$] (C)

$1\frac{5}{8} = \frac{13}{8}$
$\frac{13}{8} - \frac{2}{8} = 1\frac{3}{8}$

3. Imani completed a 200-meter race in 25.06 seconds. Talia completed the same race in 1.17 fewer seconds. How long (*l*) did it take Talia to complete the race?

Type of comparison: additive

Equation and answer: 23.89

Imani [25.06]
Talia [?] (1.17)

4. A high school has 1,446 students enrolled. A middle school has $\frac{1}{6}$ as many students enrolled as the high school. How many students (*m*) are enrolled in the middle school?

Type of comparison: multiplicative

Equation and answer: 2415

$1,446 \div \frac{1}{6} = m$, $m = 2415$ students

$296,943$
$- 155,416$
$141,527$

► Practice

Write an equation and use it to solve the problem.
Draw a model if you need to.

5. At the time of the 2010 Ohio census, 155,416 more people
   lived in Cincinnati than lived in Dayton. How many people (p)
   lived in Dayton if 296,943 people lived in Cincinnati?

$296,943$
$- 155,416$ $k = 141,527$

6. A woodworking machine decreased the thickness of a board
   from $\frac{3}{4}$ of an inch to $\frac{9}{16}$ of an inch. By what number of inches (i)
   did the thickness of the board decrease?

7. The area of Alondra's home is 9 times the area of the
   family room in her home. The family room has an area of
   192 square feet. What is the area of Alondra's home (h)?

8. Tyler has saved $14.25 of his allowance. He would like to buy a
   computer game that costs $15.70 more than the amount he has
   saved. What is the cost (c) of the game?

9. To prepare for a test, Esmeralda studied for 40 minutes.
   Mallory studied for 50 minutes. How many times (t) as
   long as Mallory did Esmeralda study?

10. A flagpole has a height of 3.2 meters. A nearby tree has an
    height of 25.6 meters. When compared to the flagpole, how
    many times as tall (t) is the tree?

11. A school fundraiser collected $776. Sun-Woo's class collected
    $\frac{1}{16}$ of that amount. What amount of money (m) was collected
    by Sun-Woo's class?

Types of Comparison Problems

CA CC Content Standards 5.OA.1, 5.NBT.5, 5.NBT.7,
5.NF.2, 5.NF.6, 5.NF.7c
Mathematical Practices MP.1, MP.3, MP.4, MP.6

► Write Equations

Write and solve an equation to find the amount of money each student spent at the school bookstore.

1. Takumi: 1 eraser for $0.59 and 6 pencils for $0.15 each

   Equation: $0.59 + (6 \times 0.15) = j$

   Answer: $j = \$1.49$

2. Jasmine: 8 book covers for $0.90 each and 1 pen for $0.49

   Equation: $(8 \times 0.90) + 0.49 = k$

   Answer: $k = \$7.69$

3. Dalton: 12 notebooks for $1.75 each and 1 marker for $1.59

   Equation: $(12 \times 1.75) + 1.59 = g$

   Answer: $g = \$22.59$

4. Jimena: 1 compass for $2.50 and 6 portfolios for $1.25 each

   Equation: $(6 \times 1.25) + 2.50 = m$

   Answer: $m = \$10$

5. Todd: 3 watercolor brushes for $2.39 each and a pencil sharpener for $0.89

   Equation: $(3 \times 2.39) + 0.89 = a$

   Answer: $a = 8.06$

► Solve Equations With Parentheses

Solve each equation.

6. $(5 \cdot 60) - 2 = n$ $n = 298$

7. $2.5 + (4 \div 0.1) = b$ $b = 42.5$

8. $3 \cdot \left(1\frac{1}{2} - \frac{1}{8}\right) = z$ $z = 4\frac{1}{8}$

9. $\left(2 \div \frac{1}{4}\right) - 1 = v$ $v = 7$

10. $\left(1\frac{3}{4} \div 3\right) + \frac{1}{4} = c$ $c = 5\frac{1}{2}$

11. $10 + \left(\frac{2}{3} \cdot 6\right) = h$ $h = 14$

12. $1.55 - (0.7 \cdot 2) = r$ $r = 0.15$

13. $(0.01 \cdot 100) - 1 = w$ $w = 0$

Name _____   Date _____

▶ Solve Two-Step Word Problems

Solve.

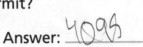

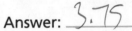

Show your work.

14. A suburban shopping mall has 105 rows of parking spaces with 45 spaces in each row. A special permit is required to park in 630 of those spaces. How many spaces (s) do not require a special permit?

Equation: _____   Answer: 4098

15. A recipe that makes 6 servings requires $1\frac{1}{4}$ cups of flour. How much flour (f) would be needed to make the recipe for one-half the number of servings?

Equation: _____   Answer: 3.75

16. An apple orchard in Minnesota has 8 rows of 26 honeycrisp trees and 14 rows of 23 red delicious trees. How many honeycrisp and red delicious trees (t) are in the orchard?

Equation: _____   Answer: 530

17. An investor purchased 250 shares of stock. Calculate the investor's total cost (c) if the price per share was $18.40 and a fee of $65.75 was charged for the transaction.

Equation: _____   Answer: 4637.5

18. An orange grove in Florida has 865 ambersweet trees and 32 rows of 40 sunstar trees. How many more (m) sunstar than ambersweet trees does the orchard have?

Equation: _____   Answer: 415

19. A manufacturing facility records the time its employees work each week in fractions of an hour.

Taliyah W. $25\frac{1}{2}$ hr   Avery S. $7\frac{3}{4}$ hr   Claire N. $39\frac{1}{4}$ hr

How many more hours (h) did Claire work than the combined hours of Taliyah and Avery?

Equation: _____   Answer: 6

Equations and Parentheses

▶ Too Much or Too Little Information

Solve each problem if possible. If a problem has too much
information, identify the extra information. If a problem has
too little information, describe the information that is needed
to solve the problem.

Show your work.

Meiling is reading a 228-page book. Yesterday she read the
first 41 pages of the book. Today she read the next 13 pages.
Her goal tomorrow is to read 10 pages. How many pages of
the book have not been read?

20. What information is not needed to solve the problem?

Her goal for tommorow

21. Write the information that is needed to solve the problem.
Then solve the problem.

The students in Mr. Westgate's class have been arranged in equal
groups for an activity. There are four students in each group.

22. How many students are participating in the activity?

Multiples of four (No. of groups x 4)

To prepare for a math test, Kelsey studied for $\frac{1}{2}$ hr, ~~Lila studied for~~
~~$\frac{3}{4}$ hr,~~ Ricardo studied for $\frac{1}{3}$ hr, and Marcus studied for 1 hour. Did
Marcus study longer than the combined times of Ricardo and Kelsey?

23. What information is not needed to solve the problem?

24. Write the information that is needed to solve the problem.
Then solve the problem and explain your answer.

$1 - \left(\frac{1}{2} + \frac{1}{3}\right) =$

Name _____ **Date** _____

▶ Practice Problem Solving

Solve each problem if possible. If a problem has too much information, identify the extra information. If a problem has too little information, describe the information that is needed to solve the problem.

25. A wallpaper border is being pasted on the walls of a rectangular room that measures 12 feet by $14\frac{1}{2}$ feet. The cost of the border is $6.50 per foot. How many feet of border is needed for the room?

 ~~17 feet~~ 26.5 ft.

_____

26. Ms. Bleyleven has 11 windows in her house. The heights in centimeters of 4 windows are shown below.

160.2 cm   163 cm   155.9 cm   158.5 cm

How many windows in her house have a height that is a whole number of centimeters?

too little information

_____

27. Anja has worked at her job for $6\frac{1}{2}$ years. Each year she works 48 weeks, and each week she works $37\frac{1}{2}$ hours. How many hours does Anja work each year?

1800

_____

28. During a driving vacation, a car was refueled 5 times. At the beginning of the vacation, the car odometer read 19,417 miles, and read 21,068 miles at the end of the vacation. How many gallons of fuel were needed to drive that number of miles?

_____

_____

Equations and Parentheses

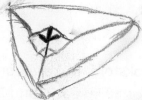

▶ Solve Multistep Problems

Solve.

Show your work.

1. An investor purchased 150 shares of stock at $13.60 per share, and sold the shares later for $11.92 per share. Calculate the profit or loss of the transaction.

   a. What equation can be used to find the amount of money needed to buy (*b*) the shares?

   _____

   b. What equation can be used to find the amount of money received for selling (*s*) the shares?

   _____

   c. Does the transaction represent a profit or loss? Why?

   _____

   d. What equation can be used to calculate the loss (*l*)? Solve your equation to calculate the loss.

   _____

2. A soccer team plays 10 games each season. Last season the team scored an average of 2.5 goals per game in its first six games, and 3.25 goals per game in its final four games. How many goals (*g*) were scored by the team last season?

   _____

3. The charge for an automobile repair was $328.50 for parts and $64 per hour for labor. The repair took $3\frac{3}{4}$ hours. What was the total cost (*c*) of the repair?

   _____

4. An auditorium has 215 rows of seats with 35 seats in each row. A reservation is required to sit in the first 6 seats of 75 rows. How many seats (*s*) do not require a reservation?

Solve.

Show your work.

5. At the school bookstore, Dakota purchased a notebook for $3.75, 6 pencils for $0.20 each, and 2 pens for $1.19 each. By what amount (*a*) was cost of the pens greater than the cost of the pencils?

_____

6. A grocery store charges $4.75 for a 26-ounce jar of peanut butter. A case of peanut butter contains 24 jars. What profit (*p*) is earned for selling 3 cases of peanut butter if the store's cost for the 3 cases is $165.90?

_____

7. This week an employee is scheduled to work $7\frac{1}{2}$ hours each day Monday through Friday, and 2 hours on Saturday morning. If the employee's goal is to work 40 hours, how many additional hours (*h*) must be worked?

_____

8. Ryan went shopping and purchased two shirts for $16 each, and a pair of sneakers that cost $2\frac{1}{2}$ times as much as a shirt. What amount of money (*m*) did Ryan spend?

_____

9. At home last night, Reza spent 35 minutes doing homework, which is 10 more minutes than Colette. Katerina worked twice as long as Colette, but 5 fewer minutes than Orvis. How long (*l*) did Orvis spend doing homework last night?

_____

10. At closing time, 55 adults and 89 students are waiting in line to ride an amusement park roller coaster. The capacity of the coaster is 38 riders. How many trips (*t*) must the coaster make to give all of the people in line a ride? How many people will be on the last trip of the day?

_____

Discuss Multistep Problems

Name _____ **Date** _____

CA CC Content Standards 5.NBT.6, 5.NF.2, 5.NF.6, NF.7c
Mathematical Practices MP.1, MP.3, MP.4, MP.6

► Practice Problem Solving

Solve each problem.   *Show your work.*

1. Four college roommates drove 1,050 miles to Florida for spring break. Xavier drove 300 more miles than Yuri, and Yuri drove 200 more miles than Zack, who drove 60 miles. How many miles did Walter (*w*) drive?

   a. How many miles did Zack drive?   _____

   b. What expression represents the miles Yuri drove?   _____

   c. What expression represents the miles Xavier drove? _____

   d. The number of miles Walter (*w*) drove is the number of miles Zack, Yuri, and Xavier drove subtracted from the number of miles the friends drove altogether. Write an equation to represent this fact.

   _____

   e. How many miles did Walter drive?   _____

2. Sasha earns $8 per hour working at her grandparents' farm. During July, she worked $39\frac{1}{2}$ hours at the farm, and earned $47 babysitting. How many more dollars (*d*) does Sasha need to earn to buy a gadget that costs $399?

   _____

3. Anya, Jose, Cali, and Stephan walk for exercise. Anya's route is $2\frac{1}{4}$ kilometers long. Jose's route is $1\frac{1}{2}$ fewer km. Cali's route is $1\frac{1}{2}$ times as long as Jose's route, and 2 fewer km than Stephan's route. What distance (*d*) is Stephan's route?

   _____

4. A $750 gift was shared equally by 5 people. After spending $90 of her share, Clarissa divided the amount remaining into 2 equal parts. What amount of money does each part (*p*) represent?

   _____

Solve each problem.

Show your work.

5. Chloe purchased a sweater that cost $24, and a shirt that cost $\frac{5}{8}$ times as much as the sweater. What amount of change (c) did Chloe receive if she gave the clerk $50?

_____

6. Matti has 1 more pencil than Chang-Lin. Renaldo has 3 times as many pencils as Chang-Lin, and 1 more than Jorge. Jorge has 5 pencils. How many pencils (p) does Matti have?

_____

7. Six teachers, seventy-eight students, and ten parents are boarding buses for a school field trip. Each bus can carry 32 passengers. If the passengers board each bus until it is full, how many passengers (p) will be on the bus that is not full?

_____

▶ What's the Error?

Dear Math Students,

I was asked to find the amount of change (c) a shopper would receive from $40 after purchasing a pair of jeans for $28 and a pair of socks that cost $\frac{1}{4}$ as much as the jeans. I used the solution equation $c = 40 - 28 - (28 \div \frac{1}{4})$ to solve the problem.

The equation did not give me a sensible answer. Can you tell me what I did wrong?

Your friend,
Puzzled Penguin

8. Write a response to Puzzled Penguin.

_____

_____

_____

Practice Problem Solving

► Math and Gymnastics

In a gymnastics competition, gymnasts compete in events such as the balance beam, parallel bars, vault, and floor exercise.

Leigh earned the following scores from the judges for her balance beam routine.

   9.20   9.30   9.20   9.30   9.20   9.00

Follow these steps to find Leigh's final score.

1. Order the scores from least to greatest.

   _____

2. Cross off the lowest score and the highest score.

   _____

3. Find the average of the remaining scores by adding the scores and dividing the sum by 4.

   _____

4. Calculate Leigh's final score by adding 7.0 (the difficulty rating of her routine) to the average you found in Exercise 3.

   _____

The judges' scores for Olivia's balance beam routine are shown below.

   9.40   9.40   9.50   9.50   9.40   9.40

5. Calculate Olivia's average score by following the steps described in Exercises 1–3 above.

   _____

6. Calculate Olivia's final score by adding 6.6 (the difficulty of her routine) to the average you found in Exercise 5.

   _____

▶ Math and Diving

In diving competitions, divers compete in springboard and platform events.

Follow these steps to find the total score for a dive.

▶ Order the judges' scores from least to greatest.

▶ Cross off the lowest score and the highest score.

▶ Find the sum of the remaining scores.

▶ Multiply the sum by the difficulty of the dive.

7. Suppose a diver earned the following scores from judges on his first of five platform dives.

    9.5   10.0   9.0   10.0   10.0

   a. In the space at the right, sketch a bar graph to display the scores.

   b. The difficulty of the dive was 3.8. Follow the steps above to calculate the total score for the dive.

   _____

8. The table below shows the scores the diver received from the judges for his four remaining dives.

Dive	Scores	Difficulty
2	9.4 8.9 9.0 9.5 9.4	3.2
3	8.8 8.6 8.0 8.0 8.5	3.5
4	9.6 9.5 9.5 9.6 9.4	2.8
5	7.0 7.5 6.5 7.5 7.0	3.0

For each dive, follow the steps above to calculate the dive's total score.

   a. Dive 2 total score: _____   b. Dive 3 total score: _____

   c. Dive 4 total score: _____   d. Dive 5 total score: _____

9. How many points altogether were scored on the five dives?

_____

Focus on Mathematical Practices

1. The model represents the length of a whale (*w*) and the length of a porpoise (*p*). For numbers 1a–1d, select True or False for the statement.

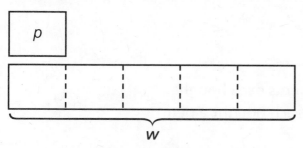

1a. The whale is 5 times as long as the porpoise.   ○ True   ○ False

1b. The porpoise is 5 times as long as the whale.   ○ True   ○ False

1c. The whale is $\frac{1}{5}$ as long as the porpoise.   ○ True   ○ False

1d. The porpoise is $\frac{1}{5}$ as long as the whale.   ○ True   ○ False

Write a word problem for the equation.

2. $\frac{1}{2} \cdot 3 = \frac{3}{2}$

3. $\frac{5}{8} \cdot 2 = \frac{10}{8}$

4. $\frac{1}{2} \div 3 = \frac{1}{6}$

5. Write a word problem for $5 \div \frac{1}{8} = 40$.

6. Five students bought supplies. Two students each bought
   2 pencils and an eraser. Three students each bought a pen
   and 3 pencils.

Supply	Cost
pencil	$0.15
eraser	$0.59
pen	$0.49

   Select the equation that can be used to find the total cost (c)
   of the supplies. Mark all that apply.

   Ⓐ $c = 2 \times 0.15 + 0.59 + 0.49 + 3 \times 0.15$
   Ⓑ $c = 2 \times (2 \times 0.15 + 0.59) + 3 \times (0.49 + 3 \times 0.15)$
   Ⓒ $c = 13 \times 0.15 + 2 \times 0.59 + 3 \times 0.49$
   Ⓓ $c = 2 \times (0.15 + 0.59) + 3 \times (0.49 + 0.15)$
   Ⓔ $c = 4 \times 0.15 + 2 \times 0.59 + 3 \times 0.49 + 9 \times 0.15$
   Ⓕ $c = 2 \times (2 \times 0.15 + 0.59) + 3 \times (0.49 + 0.15)$

7. Students in the high school marching band are arranged in
   17 equal rows. There are 85 students in the marching band.

   Part A

   How many students are in each row? Write an equation and
   use it to solve the problem.

   Part B

   Explain how you know your answer is reasonable.

8. Penn volunteered a total of 72 hours over the last 12 weeks. He volunteered the same number of hours each week.

   Part A

   How many hours did Penn volunteer in one week? Write an equation and use it to solve the problem.

   _____

   Part B

   Explain how you know your answer is reasonable.

   _____

9. Henry has $2\frac{3}{4}$ cups of flour. He uses $1\frac{1}{2}$ cups of the flour to bake muffins. How much flour (*f*) does Henry have left?

   Part A

   Complete the model to represent this problem.

   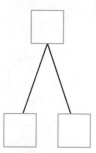

   Part B

   Write an equation. Then solve.

   _____

Without solving the problem, choose the words that make the sentence true.

10. Fido eats 2 cups of kibble. Fifi eats $\frac{6}{5}$ of what Fido eats.

    Fifi eats | more than / less than / the same as | Fido.

© Houghton Mifflin Harcourt Publishing Company

11. Camille collects stickers. Her sticker book holds 5 stickers in each row. When a page is full, it holds 65 stickers. How many rows (*r*) of stickers are on a full page?

Part A

Complete the model to represent this problem.

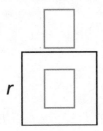

Part B

Write an equation. Then solve.

12. Julianne and Derek made signs for their school spirit week. Julianne made a sign that is $3\frac{1}{2}$ feet long. Derek made a sign that is $\frac{5}{6}$ as long as Julianne's sign. How long is the sign Derek made? Complete the equation.

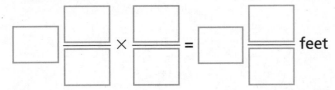 feet

13. Emilio made 65 potholders. Each potholder cost him $1.65 to make. If he sells each potholder for $2.12, how much profit will he make?

$_____

14. Without multiplying the numbers, classify the expression as *less than 3.75* or *greater than 3.75*. Write the letter of the expression in the appropriate box.

Ⓐ $3\frac{3}{4} \times \frac{9}{10}$ Ⓑ 1.2×3.75 Ⓒ $2 \times 3\frac{3}{4}$ Ⓓ $3\frac{3}{4} \times \frac{1}{2}$ Ⓔ 3.75×0.75

Less than 3.75	Greater than 3.75

15. Mr. and Mrs. Storey drove 3,200 miles during their vacation.
Mr. Storey (y) drove 3 times as many miles as Mrs. Storey (x).

Part A

Draw a model to represent the problem.

Part B

How many miles did each person drive?

16. At an electronics store, a refrigerator costs 3 times as much as a
DVD player. A dishwasher costs $125 more than a DVD player.

Part A

Use the numbers to complete the sign.

Item	Price
DVD player	$150
Refrigerator	$ ☐☐☐
Dishwasher	$ ☐☐☐

0   2

4   5

6   7

Part B

Mrs. Shin bought 12 refrigerators and 12 dishwashers for her
apartment building. She received a discount of $90 on the entire
purchase. Write an equation using parentheses to find the amount she
owes. Then solve.

17. For numbers 17a–17e, choose Yes or No to indicate whether the comparison is additive.

17a. 250 times as long   ○ Yes   ○ No

17b. 123 more than   ○ Yes   ○ No

17c. $2.56 less than   ○ Yes   ○ No

17d. in $\frac{1}{2}$ the time   ○ Yes   ○ No

17e. 3.2 fewer seconds   ○ Yes   ○ No

18. Jerome scores 12 points in a basketball game. This is twice the number of points that Jaime scores. How many points did the rest of the team score? Solve the problem if possible. Identify extra information or information that is needed to solve the problem.

19. A car is 234 inches long. A model of the car is $\frac{1}{18}$ times the size of the actual car. Without solving the problem, select the answer that is the most reasonable length of the model of the car.

Ⓐ $\frac{13}{18}$ inches

Ⓑ 13 inches

Ⓒ 216 inches

Ⓓ 4,212 inches

20. A python (p) is 1.5 feet longer than a boa constrictor (b). Choose an expression from each column to create an equation that compares the lengths of the snakes.

○ $b + 1.5$		○ $p - 1.5$
○ $1.5b$	=	○ $1.5p$
○ b		○ $p + 1.5$
○ $b - 1.5$		○ p

Family Letter

Content Overview

Dear Family,

In our math class, we are studying algebra and operations. Your child will explore simplifying expressions using the Order of Operations.

Your child will generate ordered pairs and use the first quadrant of the coordinate plane to graph the *x*- and *y*-coordinates. An example is shown below.

x	1	2	3	4
y	4	8	12	16

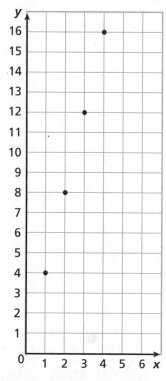

You can be an active part of your child's learning by asking your child to provide answers or examples for the following questions:

- What algebraic expression describes, "4 more than the product of 2 and *c*?"
- Generate the first five terms of a pattern with the rule *Add 5*.
- For the ordered pair (4, 6), which is the *x*-coordinate and which is the *y*-coordinate?

Sincerely,
Your child's teacher

 CA CC

Unit 7 addresses the following standards from the *Common Core State Standards for Mathematics with California Additions*: **5.0A.1, 5.0A.2, 5.0A.2.1, 5.0A.3, 5.G.1, 5.G.2**, and all Mathematical Practices.

Un vistazo general al contenido

Estimada familia:

En nuestra clase de matemáticas, estamos estudiando álgebra y operaciones. Su niño aprenderá cómo simplificar expresiones usando el Orden de las operaciones.

Su niño generará pares ordenados y usará el primer cuadrante del plano de coordenadas para hacer una gráfica de la coordenada *x*- y de la coordenada *y*-. Abajo se muestra un ejemplo.

x	1	2	3	4
y	4	8	12	16

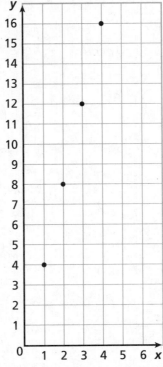

Usted puede participar activamente en el aprendizaje de su niño, pidiéndole que responda las siguientes preguntas:

- ¿Qué expresión algebraica describe "4 más que el producto de 2 por *c*"?
- Genera los primeros cinco términos de un patrón, usando la regla *"Suma 5"*.
- Para el par ordenado (4, 6), ¿cuál es la coordenada *x* y cuál es la coordenada *y*?

Atentamente,
El maestro de su niño

 CA CC

En la Unidad 7 se aplican los siguientes estándares auxiliares, contenidos en los *Estándares estatales comunes de matemáticas con adiciones para California*: **5.OA.1, 5.OA.2, 5.OA.2.1, 5.OA.3, 5.G.1, 5.G.2** y todos los de prácticas matemáticas.

Read and Write Expressions

▶ Simple Expressions

Below are some **expressions**. Expressions do not have equal signs.

$\frac{1}{2} + \frac{2}{3}$ 　　 $24 \div 3$ 　　 $5 \cdot (6 - 2)$ 　　 $6 + n$ 　　 $12 - 10 \times 0.4$

Expressions use numbers and symbols to "express" computations.

Expression	Computation in Words
$3.5 + 6.3$	Add 3.5 and 6.3.
$10 - 2$	Subtract 2 from 10.
$\frac{1}{2} \cdot p$	Multiply p by $\frac{1}{2}$.
$14 \div 4$	Divide 14 by 4.

There is more than one way to say some of the computations above. For example, for $3.5 + 6.3$, you also could say, "Find the sum of 3.5 and 6.3."

1. What is another way to say $\frac{1}{2} \cdot p$? _____

Write the computation in words.

2. $7.5 - 2.25$ _____

3. $b + 9$ _____

4. $\frac{3}{4} \cdot 8 \cdot \frac{1}{2}$ _____

5. $1.6 \div 0.2$ _____

Write an expression for the words.

6. Find the product of 12 and 0.1. 12×0.1

7. Subtract $\frac{2}{3}$ from $3\frac{1}{2}$. $3\frac{1}{2} - \frac{2}{3}$

8. Add 14 and t. $14 + t$

9. Divide p by q. $p \div q$

VOCABULARY
Order of Operations

▶ Expressions with More than One Operation

When you read and write expressions with more than
one operation, think about the **Order of Operations**.

$11 \cdot 15 + 3$	Multiply 11 and 15 and then add 3.
$11 \cdot (15 + 3)$	Add 15 and 3 and then multiply by 11.

Order of Operations
Step 1 Perform operations inside parentheses.
Step 2 Multiply and divide from left to right.
Step 3 Add and subtract from left to right.

10. Consider the expression $12 \div (5 + 2)$.

    a. Which operation is done first, division or addition?

    division _____

    b. Write the computation in words.

    _____

11. Consider the expression $12 \div 5 + 2$.

    a. Which operation is done first, division or addition?

    division _____

    b. Write the computation in words.

    _____

Write the computation in words. Think about the Order of Operations.

12. $3.5 - (2.1 + 1.2)$ _____

13. $\frac{1}{2} + \frac{3}{4} \cdot t$ _____

14. $(25 - 10) \div 5$ _____

Write an expression for the words. Think about the Order of Operations.

15. Multiply the sum of p and 3 by 0.1 $(3+p) \times 0.1$ _____

16. Divide 36 by 4 and then add 3. $(36 \div 4) + 3$ _____

17. Add the product of 2 and 5 to the product of 9 and 8.

    $(2 \times 5) + (9 \times 8)$ _____

Name _____   **Date** _____

CA CC Content Standards **5.OA.1**
Mathematical Practices **MP.3, MP.6, MP.7**

VOCABULARY
simplify

► Simplify Expressions

If an expression does not have a letter, or variable, then you can **simplify** it to find its value. For example, you can simplify $15 \div 3$ to get 5.

How do you simplify an expression that has more than one operation? For example, when you simplify $12 - 3 \cdot 2$, do you subtract first or multiply first?

The Order of Operations tells us that to simplify $12 - 3 \cdot 2$, we multiply first and then subtract.

$$12 - 3 \cdot 2 = 12 - 6 \qquad \text{Multiply.}$$
$$= 6 \qquad\qquad \text{Subtract.}$$

Order of Operations
Step 1 Perform operations inside parentheses.
Step 2 Multiply and divide from left to right.
Step 3 Add and subtract from left to right.

1. Follow the Order of Operations to simplify $25 - (5 + 2) \cdot 3$.

    Step 1 Perform operations inside parentheses. _____

    Step 2 Multiply and divide from left to right. _____

    Step 3 Add and subtract from left to right. _____

Simplify. Follow the Order of Operations.

2. $5 + 16 \div 4$

3. $10 \cdot (0.3 + 0.2)$

4. $20 \div 4 + 3 \cdot 3$

5. $\left(\frac{5}{6} - \frac{1}{3}\right) \cdot 4$

6. $21 - 12 + 9 - 2$

7. $6 \times (2 + 4) \div 3$

8. $0.3 + 0.1 \cdot 5 + 0.2$

9. $18 + 9 \div 0.1$

10. $36 \div 3 \cdot 2$

► Grouping Symbols

Parentheses group parts of an expression together and let you
know which operations to do first. Brackets, [ ], and braces, { },
are also grouping symbols. These symbols are often used when
an expression has grouping symbols inside other grouping symbols.

To simplify an expression with grouping symbols inside
other grouping symbols, work from the inside out.

$$12 \cdot [48 \div (4 + 4)] = 12 \cdot [48 \div 8] \quad \text{Add inside the parentheses.}$$
$$= 12 \cdot 6 \qquad\qquad \text{Divide inside the brackets.}$$
$$= 72 \qquad\qquad\quad \text{Multiply.}$$

Simplify.

11. $6 \cdot (12 - 4) \div 16$

    $48 \div 16$

12. $(1 - \frac{2}{3}) \times (1 - \frac{2}{3})$

    $\frac{1}{3} * \frac{1}{3}$

13. $(1.3 + 2.7) \div (2.2 - 1.7)$

    $4 \div 0.5$

14. $50 - [40 - (30 - 20)]$

    $60 - 30$

15. $100 \div [(12 - 7) \cdot 2]$

    $100 \div 10$

16. $10 - \{8 \div [4 \div (2 \div 1)]\}$

    $10 - 4$

► What's the Error?

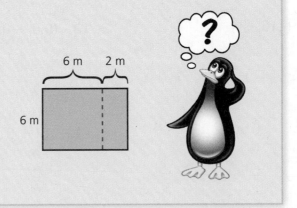

Dear Math Students,

I wrote the expression 6 • 6 + 2 for
the area of the rectangle at the
right. My friend said, "You forgot
the parentheses." Can you explain
what my friend meant?

Your friend,
Puzzled Penguin

17. Write a response to Puzzled Penguin.

_____

_____

_____

Simplify Expressions

Name   **Date**

CA CC Content Standards **5.OA.1, 5.OA.2**
Mathematical Practices **MP.1, MP.4, MP.8**

VOCABULARY
evaluate
variable

▶ Expressions with Variables

The expressions below contain letters, or **variables**.
A variable represents an unknown number.

$$3\tfrac{1}{2} + x \quad n \div 0.01 \quad 5 \cdot (p - 2) \quad t - 6 \quad 4 + 10 \times w$$

To **evaluate** an expression, substitute a value for the variable and then use the Order of Operations to simplify.

Evaluate $5 \cdot (p - 2)$ for $p = 10$.

$5 \cdot (p - 2) = 5 \cdot (10 - 2)$	Substitute 10 for p.
$= 5 \cdot 8$	Subtract inside parentheses.
$= 40$	Multiply.

Order of Operations

Step 1 Perform operations inside parentheses.

Step 2 Multiply and divide from left to right.

Step 3 Add and subtract from left to right.

Evaluate the expression.

1. $m - 4.7$ for $m = 10$

2. $5 \div x$ for $x = \tfrac{1}{3}$

3. $5 + n \cdot 4$ for $n = 3$

4. $\tfrac{1}{5} \cdot x$ for $x = 15$

5. $7.5 \times (d - 2.5)$ for $d = 3.5$

6. $48 \div (z - 6)$ for $z = 14$

7. $10 \cdot (0.05 + q)$ for $q = 1.2$

8. $2\tfrac{3}{4} + d - 1\tfrac{1}{4} + 5\tfrac{1}{2}$ for $d = 1\tfrac{1}{2}$

9. $1{,}000 \cdot h$ for $h = 0.004$

10. $(t + 18) \div 5$ for $t = 17$

11. $54 \div 3 \cdot v$ for $v = 3$

12. $6 \cdot 0.01 + n \cdot 0.1$ for $n = 2$

▶ Real World Expressions

13. Four friends earned $24 by washing cars and m dollars by mowing lawns. They want to divide the total equally.

   a. Write an expression for the amount each friend gets.

   _____

   b. If they made $50 mowing lawns, how much should each friend get?

   _____

14. There are $\frac{2}{3}$ as many students in science club as in math club.

   a. If there are m students in math club, how many are in science club?

   _____

   b. If there are 27 students in math club, how many are in science club?

   _____

15. Kima's cat weighs 6 pounds more than her rabbit. Her dog weighs 3 times as much as her cat. Let r be the weight of Kima's rabbit.

   a. How much does her cat weigh?

   _____

   b. How much does her dog weigh?

   _____

   c. If Kima's rabbit weighs 5 pounds, how much do her cat and dog weigh?

   _____

16. To change a temperature from degrees Celsius to degrees Fahrenheit, multiply it by $\frac{9}{5}$ and then add 32.

   a. Let c be a temperature in degrees Celsius. Write an expression for changing c to degrees Fahrenheit.

   _____

   b. Use your expression to change 20°C to Fahrenheit degrees.

   _____

Evaluate Expressions

Name _____ **Date** _____

CA CC Content Standards **5.OA.1, 5.OA.2, 5.OA.2.1, 5.OA.3**
Mathematical Practices **MP.1, MP.2, MP.6, MP.7, MP.8**

> **VOCABULARY**
> numerical pattern
> term

▶ Patterns and Expressions

A **numerical pattern** is a sequence of numbers that share a relationship. Each number in a numerical pattern is a **term**. Below we show the first five terms of a pattern.

$$3, 5, 7, 9, 11, \ldots$$

The pattern above starts with 3, and then each term is two more than the previous term. You can write numerical expressions for the terms. We show two possible expressions for each term below.

3	5	7	9	11
↑	↑	↑	↑	↑

Expressions $\begin{cases} 3 & 3+2 & 3+2+2 & 3+2+2+2 & 3+2+2+2+2 \\ 3 & 3+(1 \cdot 2) & 3+(2 \cdot 2) & 3+(3 \cdot 2) & 3+(4 \cdot 2) \end{cases}$

Solve.

1. a. Write two expressions for the next term (the sixth term) in the pattern 3, 5, 7, 9, 11 . . .

    _11+2_
    _2+11_

    b. Write the next term. _13_

2. a. Write the first five terms of a numerical pattern that begins with 5 and then adds 5.

    _5, 10, 15, 20, 25_

    b. Write an expression for the sixth term of the pattern.

    _25+5_

    c. Write the sixth term. _30_

3. a. Write the first five terms of a numerical pattern that begins with 1 and then adds 9.

    _1, 10, 19, 28, 37_

    b. Write an expression for the sixth term of the pattern.

    _36+9=54_

    c. Write the sixth term. _54_

► Patterns and Relationships

Solve.

4. a. Write the first five terms of a pattern that begins with 2, and then adds 2.

   b. Write the first five terms of a pattern that begins with 4, and then adds 4.

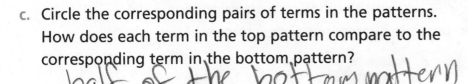

   c. Circle the corresponding pairs of terms in the patterns. How does each term in the top pattern compare to the corresponding term in the bottom pattern?
   half of the bottom pattern

   d. How does the bottom term compare to the top term?
   2 times greater

5. a. Write the first five terms of a pattern that begins with 9, and then adds 9.

   9 18 27 36 45

   b. Write the first five terms of a pattern that begins with 3, and then adds 3.

   3 6 9 12 15

   c. Circle the corresponding pairs of terms in the patterns. How does each term in the top pattern compare to the corresponding term in the bottom pattern?
   3 times greater

   d. How does the bottom term compare to the top term?
   1/3 of top row

6. a. Write the first five terms of two different patterns.

   8 16 24 32 40
   3 6 9 12 15

   b. Describe two different relationships that the corresponding terms of your patterns share.

   _____

   _____

Patterns and Relationships

► Real World Patterns

Many situations in your everyday life can be described by numerical patterns. The table below shows late fees for an overdue library book. Complete the table.

Overdue Book Late Fee					
Number of Days Late	1	2	3	4	5
Late Fee	15¢	30¢	45¢	60¢	75

7. Describe the relationship between the corresponding terms.

_____

_____

Complete the table and describe the relationship between corresponding terms.

8.

Bicycles and Wheels					
Bicycles	1	2	3	4	5
Wheels	2	4	6	8	10

_____

9.

Cost of Concert Tickets					
Tickets	1	2	3	4	5
Cost in Dollars	35	70	105	175	140

switch

_____

_____

10.

Weather Relationships					
Inches of Rain	0	0.5	1	1.5	2
Inches of Snow	0	5	10	15	20

_____

Name _____   Date _____

VOCABULARY
prime number

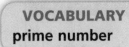

► Is It Prime?

A **prime number** is a number greater than 1 that has 1 and itself as the only factors. A composite number is a number greater than 1 that has more than two factors.

You can write an expression for any number using only prime factors.

Examples: 13   1 • 13 (13 is a prime number. It has exactly two factors)

24   2 • 2 • 2 • 3 (24 is a composite number. It has more than two factors)

Write the factors in order from least to greatest.

1. Write all the one-digit numbers that are prime.

_____

2. Write all the two-digit numbers less than 20 that are prime.

_____

Write an expression for the number using prime factors.

3. 8
2+2x2+2

4. 18
(2x3)x3

5. 35
7x5

6. 30
(3x5)+(3x5)

7. 22
11+11

8. 28
23+5

9. 36
31+5

10. 27
29-2

11. 40
43-40

Write prime or composite next to each number.

12. 29
prime

13. 36
composite

14. 43
prime

15. 31
Prime

16. 33
composite

17. 47
prime

Patterns and Relationships

Name _____   **Date** _____

CA CC Content Standards **5.G.1**
Mathematical Practices **MP.1, MP.2, MP.3, MP.5, MP.6, MP.7, MP.8**

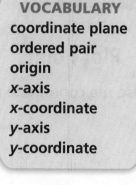

VOCABULARY
coordinate plane
ordered pair
origin
x-axis
x-coordinate
y-axis
y-coordinate

► Read Points

A **coordinate plane** is formed by the intersection of a horizontal number line, called the **x-axis**, and a vertical number line, called the **y-axis**.

Use the coordinate plane below to answer the questions.

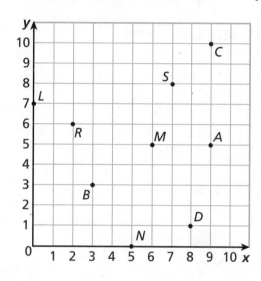

1. An **ordered pair** is used to describe the location of any point in the coordinate plane. For example, the ordered pair (9, 5) describes the location of point *A*. An ordered pair consists of two **coordinates**.

   a. The first coordinate represents distance along which axis?

   _____

   b. The second coordinate represents distance along which axis?

   _____

2. The **origin** of the coordinate plane is the point at (0, 0). Why is the origin an important point?

   _____

   _____

Write an ordered pair to represent the location of each point.

3. point *B* _____

4. point *C* _____

5. point *D* _____

6. point *L* _____

7. point *M* _____

8. point *N* _____

9. point *R* _____

10. point *S* _____

▶ Plot Points

Use the coordinate plane below to complete Exercises 11–25.

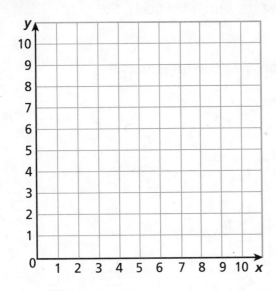

Plot and label a point at each location.

11. point *J* at (5, 4)

12. point *Q* at (1, 9)

13. point *Y* at (2, 0)

14. point *W* at (0, 4)

15. point *K* at (4, 5)

16. point *R* at (8, 3)

17. point *B* at (6, 1)

18. point *V* at (3, 8)

19. point *L* at (10, 0)

20. point *P* at (7, 10)

21. point *C* at (0, 6)

22. point *Z* at (9, 7)

**On the coordinate plane above, draw an angle of the given type.
The angle should have its vertex at one labeled point and sides that
pass through two other labeled points. Give the name of the angle.**

23. acute angle _____

24. obtuse angle _____

25. right angle _____

The Coordinate Plane

► Horizontal and Vertical Distance

26. Plot a point at (1, 10). Label the point *A*.
    Plot a point at (1, 7). Label the point *B*.
    Plot a point at (8, 10). Label the point *C*.
    Plot a point at (8, 7). Label the point *D*.
    Connect the points to form a quadrilateral.

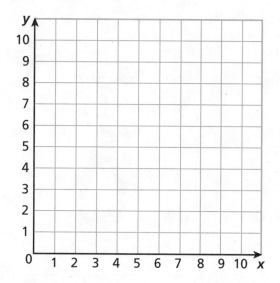

27. Explain how subtraction can be used to find the lengths of line segments *AB* and *AC*.

    _____

    _____

    _____

    _____

28. In the coordinate plane above, draw a rectangle that is not a square.

29. What ordered pairs represent the vertices of the rectangle?

    _____

30. Write a subtraction equation to represent the length of the rectangle, and write a subtraction equation to represent its width.

    _____

▶ What's the Error?

Dear Math Students,

I was asked to name the location of a fourth point that would form a square when the points are connected by line segments.

I think the point (7, 4) would form a square.

Do you think that is correct?

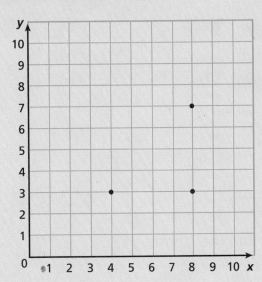

Your friend,
Puzzled Penguin

31. Write a response to Puzzled Penguin.

_____

_____

_____

_____

_____

_____

Name _____ **Date** _____

CA CC Content Standards **5.OA.3, 5.G.1, 5.G.2**
Mathematical Practices **MP.1, MP.2, MP.3, MP.4, MP.5, MP.6**

▶ Generate and Graph Ordered Pairs

Numerical patterns can be written horizontally or vertically. The *add 4* table below shows a numerical pattern in the left column and the result of adding 4 in the right column.

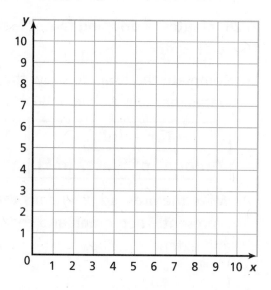

add 4	
1	5
2	
3	
4	
5	

(x, y)
(1, 5)
(___, ___)
(___, ___)
(___, ___)
(___, ___)

1. Complete the *add 4* table.

2. Complete the (x, y) table to show the ordered pairs that the *add 4* table represents.

3. Each ordered pair represents a point in the coordinate plane. Graph and connect the points.

Suppose a shrub grows at the rate shown in the table below. Use the table to complete Exercises 4 and 5.

Growth of a Shrub	
Age (years)	Height (feet)
0	0
1	1
2	2
3	3
4	4

4. Write five ordered pairs that the data represent.

_____

5. Graph the ordered pairs. What does each axis of the graph represent?

_____

_____

► Real World Problems

**In 20 minutes, a dripping faucet leaks
10 mL of water.**

6. Complete the table to show the amount of
water that will leak in 0, 40, and 60 minutes.

Time (min)	0	20	40	60
Amount of Water (mL)		10		

7. Write the ordered (x, y) pairs that the data
represent. Then graph and connect the points
and extend the line.

(___, ___) (___, ___) (___, ___) (___, ___)

8. What amount of water would you expect to
leak in 90 minutes? Explain your answer.

_____

_____

_____

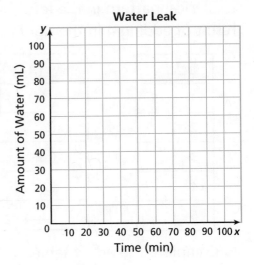

Water Leak

**The graph represents an automobile traveling
at a constant speed.**

9. The points on the graph represent four
ordered (x, y) pairs. Write the ordered pairs.

(___, ___) (___, ___) (___, ___) (___, ___)

10. Complete the table to show the relationship
between time and distance.

Time (hours)	0			
Distance (miles)	0			

11. At what constant rate of speed was the
automobile traveling? Explain how you know.

_____

_____

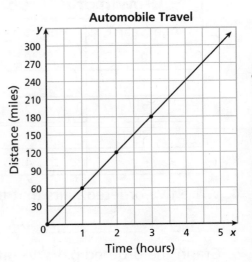

Automobile Travel

▶ Math and Constellations

An *astronomer* is a scientist who studies objects in space such as stars, planets, and galaxies.

Although you can see only a few thousand stars when you look into the night sky, astronomers have used special instruments to find and catalogue more than 800,000 different stars.

Constellations are patterns of a few bright stars that form pictures in the night sky. The well-known constellation Orion is shown at the right. Some people interpret the arrangement of stars as a hunter with a bow; others as a warrior with a shield.

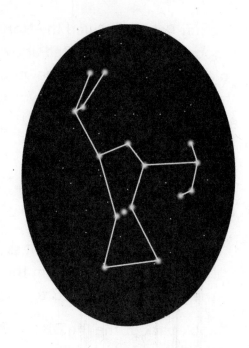

Solve.

1. The grid at the right shows the constellation Gemini. Gemini is sometimes called "The Twins." On the lines below, write the coordinates of the points that form Gemini.

   _____

   _____

   _____

   _____

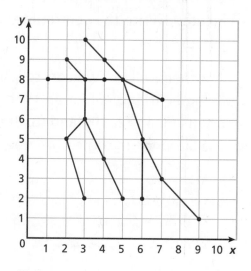

2. The points shown below form another well-known constellation that is sometimes called "The Big Dipper."

   (0, 3) (2, 4) (4, 3) (5, 2) (5, 0) (7, 0) (8, 2)

   On the grid at the right, plot the points. Then connect the points in the order in which you plotted them to form the Big Dipper.

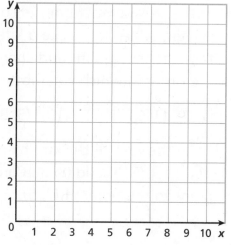

The star Polaris is called the North Star because it appears as if it is located above Earth's North Pole. Polaris is also well known because all the stars in the sky appear to revolve around it.

The picture at the right was taken by pointing a camera at Polaris and leaving the lens open for several hours.

Solve.

3. To find Polaris in the night sky, first find the Big Dipper. A ray drawn from the two stars shown at the right always points toward Polaris.

   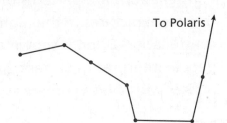

   To Polaris

   Look back at the Big Dipper you drew for Exercise 2. On the grid, draw a point where Polaris could be located. Write the coordinates of the point you drew.

4. Another well known constellation is the Summer Triangle. Plot and connect the points (5, 1), (2, 10), and (8, 8) to form the Summer Triangle. Describe the triangle.

   _____

   _____

   _____

   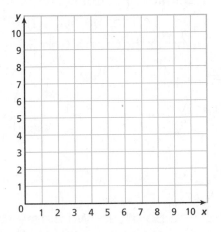

5. The points below form the constellation Bootes, which looks like a kite that has two tails. Plot the points and connect them in the order in which you plotted them.

   (7, 5) (4, 6) (2, 7) (2, 9) (5, 9) (6, 7) (7, 5)

   Form the tails of the kite by plotting points at (5, 3) and (8, 5). Connect each point to the point at (7, 5).

   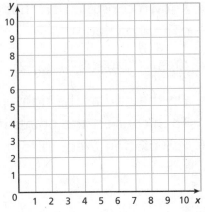

1. Use the numbers to complete the ordered pairs that represent the endpoints of line segment *RT*.

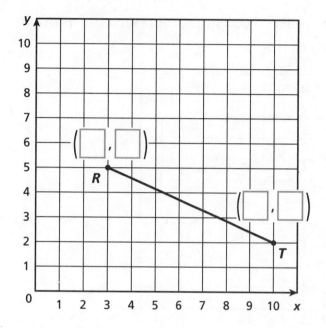

2. Place parentheses in the expression so it simplifies to 30. $5 \cdot 7 - 3 + 2$

3. Write $12.9 + 8$ using words.

4. Write $8 \div (7 - 5)$ using words.

5. Select the expression that represents adding 2 to the quotient of 12 divided by *y*. Mark all that apply.

Ⓐ $(12 \div y) + 2$ Ⓓ $12y + 2$

Ⓑ $(2 + 12) \div y$ Ⓔ $2 + 12y$

Ⓒ $2 + (12 \div y)$ Ⓕ $12 \div y + 2$

6. For numbers 6a–6c, use the Order of Operations to simplify the expression.

6a. $15 + 6 \div 3$ ☐   6b. $2 + 5 \cdot 8$ ☐   6c. $20 \div (4 + 6)$ ☐

7. The graph shows the line segment *AB*.

Part A

Write the ordered pairs that represent the endpoints of line segment *AB*.

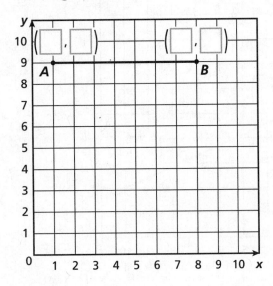

Part B

Explain how subtraction can be used to find the length of line segment *AB*.

8. For numbers 8a–8e, select True or False to indicate whether the expression represents multiplying the sum of 8 and 2 by 6.

8a. $8 + 2 \cdot 6$ ○ True   ○ False

8b. $(8 + 2) \cdot 6$ ○ True   ○ False

8c. $8 + (2 \cdot 6)$ ○ True   ○ False

8d. $6 \cdot (8 + 2)$ ○ True   ○ False

8e. $6 \cdot 8 + 2$ ○ True   ○ False

9. Write a letter in each box that shows the expressions in order from least to greatest.

A	B	C	D
$48 \div (4 - 2) + 60 \div 2$	$42 \div 7 - 3 \cdot 2$	$9 + (18 - 3) \div 0.3$	$(1.4 + 0.6) \cdot (2 - 0.4)$

☐ , ☐ , ☐ , ☐

least   greatest

10. Select one expression and one value for the variable that makes the sentence true.

Zeke got 38 when he correctly evaluated the expression ___?___ for ___?___.

Expression	Value of Variable
○ $n \div 2 + 20$	○ $n = 2$
○ $8 + n \cdot 3$	○ $n = 5$
○ $(16 - n) \cdot 4$	○ $n = 10$
○ $40 - (60 \div n)$	○ $n = 12$

11. The table shows rules for two numerical patterns.

Part A

Complete the table by writing the next four terms in each pattern.

Add 5	5				
Add 20	20				

Part B

Describe a relationship between the corresponding pairs in the two patterns.

12. The lake's water level rises 10 centimeters each day. The table shows the total change in water level for 0, 1, 2, and 3 days.

Time (days)	0	1	2	3
Total Change (cm)	0	10	20	30

Part A

Graph the data in the table.

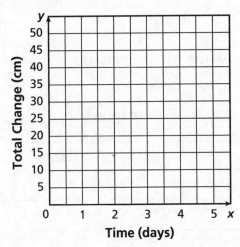

Part B

What total change in water level would you expect after 5 days? Explain your reasoning.

13. For numbers 13a–13f, choose Yes or No to indicate whether the first step in simplifying the expression is addition.

13a. $6 + 3 - 2 + 1$ ○ Yes ○ No

13b. $8.5 + 3 \cdot 4 - 2$ ○ Yes ○ No

13c. $45 \div (5 - 3) + 6$ ○ Yes ○ No

13d. $40 \div 4 \cdot (2 + 8)$ ○ Yes ○ No

13e. $45 + 4 - 2 \div 2$ ○ Yes ○ No

13f. $[25.6 - (4.5 + 2)] \cdot 1.4$ ○ Yes ○ No

14. Stephen is flying his kite. He lets out 15 feet of string each minute. Complete the table to show how much string he lets out for 1, 2, and 3 minutes. Then graph the data.

Time (minutes)	0			
Length (feet)	0			

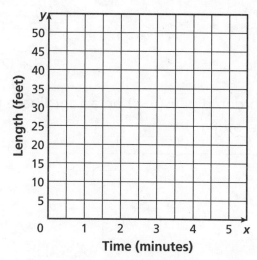

15. Tami measures the total amount of water, in liters, that flows out of her sink and tub faucets each minute they are running. Describe two different relationships that the graph displays.

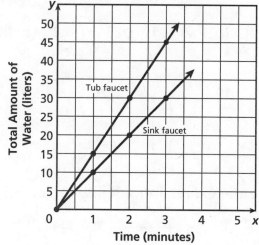

16. Draw a line to match the computation in words
to the correct expression.

Multiply the sum of 3 and 5 by 2. •   • $3 \cdot (5 + 2)$

Add the product of 2 and 3 to 5. •   • $(5 \cdot 2) + 3$

Multiply 3 by the sum of 5 and 2. •   • $(3 + 5) \cdot 2$

Add 3 to the product of 5 and 2. •   • $5 + (2 \cdot 3)$

17. Describe how to locate the ordered pair (6, 8) on a coordinate plane.
Begin your description at the origin.

18. Evaluate each expression for $n = 8$. Then classify the result as equal to
5, 10, or 20. Write the letter of the expression in the correct box.

Ⓐ $48 \div n + 4$ Ⓑ $4 \cdot (n - 3)$ Ⓒ $(n \div 2) + 1$ Ⓓ $3 \cdot n - 4$ Ⓔ $80 \div n \cdot 0.5$ Ⓕ $4 + n \div \frac{1}{2}$

5	10	20

19. Select the numbers that make the expression simplify to 36.

$$60 - \left[\begin{matrix} 1 \\ 2 \\ 3 \\ 4 \end{matrix} \cdot \left(12 - \begin{matrix} 1 \\ 2 \\ 3 \\ 4 \end{matrix} \right) \right]$$

Family Letter

Content Overview

Dear Family,

Your child is learning to convert units of measurement for length, liquid volume, and weight. Liquid volume is a measure of the amount of liquid in a container. It is measured in units such as liters or quarts.

Your child will also learn about units of weight and mass. Two objects with the same volume can have very different masses—for example, iron and wood. Weight is a measure of the pull of gravity on these objects: an object made of iron weighs more than that same object made of wood. Weight is different on Earth than on the moon, but mass always stays the same.

Volume is a measure of the space that a three-dimensional figure, such as a box, occupies. This is a new topic at this grade level.

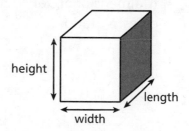

Your child will learn the underlying concepts of volume as well as multiply the three dimensions of a rectangular prism, length × width × height to find its volume. Volume is measured in cubic units, such as cubic meters or cubic feet.

Your child will also learn that attributes belonging to a category of two-dimensional figures also belong to all subcategories of that category. Students then learn to classify two-dimensional figures in a hierarchy based on properties.

If you have any questions or comments, please call or write to me.

Sincerely,
Your child's teacher

© Houghton Mifflin Harcourt Publishing Company

 CA CC

Unit 8 addresses the following standards from the *Common Core State Standards for Mathematics with California Additions*: **5.NF.4b, 5.MD.1, 5.MD.2, 5.MD.3, 5.MD.4, 5.MD.3a, 5.MD.3b, 5.MD.5, 5.MD.5a, 5.MD.5b, 5.MD.5c, 5.G.3, 5.G.4,** and all Mathematical Practices.

Estimada familia:

Su niño está aprendiendo a convertir unidades de medida de longitud, volumen de líquidos y peso. El volumen de un líquido es la medida de la cantidad de líquido en un recipiente. Se mide en unidades tales como litros o cuartos.

Su niño también aprenderá acerca de unidades de peso y de masa. Dos objetos con el mismo volumen pueden tener masas muy diferentes, por ejemplo, el hierro y la madera. El peso es la medida de la fuerza de gravedad ejercida sobre esos objetos: un objeto de hierro pesa más que el mismo objeto hecho de madera. El peso en la Tierra es diferente que el peso en la Luna, pero la masa siempre es la misma.

El volumen es la medida del espacio que una figura tridimensional, tal como una caja, ocupa. Este es un tema nuevo en este grado.

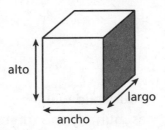

Su niño aprenderá los conceptos subyacentes de volumen, así como a multiplicar las tres medidas de un prisma rectangular: largo × ancho × alto, para hallar su volumen. El volumen se mide en unidades cúbicas, tales como metros cúbicos o pies cúbicos.

Su niño también aprenderá que los atributos que pertenecen a una categoría de figuras bidimensionales, también pertenecen a todas las subcategorías de esa categoría. Luego, los niños aprenderán a clasificar figuras bidimensionales usando una jerarquía basada en las propiedades.

Si tiene alguna pregunta o algún comentario, por favor comuníquese conmigo.

Atentamente,
El maestro de su niño

© Houghton Mifflin Harcourt Publishing Company

 CA CC

En la Unidad 8 se aplican los siguientes estándares auxiliares, contenidos en los *Estándares Estatales Comunes de Matemáticas con Adiciones para California*: **5.NF.4b, 5.MD.1, 5.MD.2, 5.MD.3, 5.MD.3a, 5.MD.3b, 5.MD.5, 5.MD.5a, 5.MD.5b, 5.MD.5c, 5.MD.4, 5.G.3, 5.G.4,** y todos los de prácticas matemáticas.

Name _____ **Date** _____

CA CC Content Standards **5.MD.1**
Mathematical Practices **MP.1, MP.2, MP.3, MP.6, MP.7**

(handwritten: 1000 × 200, 200000 0)

▶ Convert Units of Length

A meter is the basic unit of metric length. This chart shows the relationship between meters and other metric units of length.

Metric Units of Length	
1 dekameter (dam) = 10 meters	1 meter = 0.1 dekameter
1 hectometer (hm) = 100 meters	1 meter = 0.01 hectometer
1 kilometer (km) = 1,000 meters	1 meter = 0.001 kilometer
1 meter = 10 decimeters (dm)	0.1 meter = 1 decimeter
1 meter = 100 centimeters (cm)	0.01 meter = 1 centimeter
1 meter = 1,000 millimeters (mm)	0.001 meter = 1 millimeter

Example 1 **Convert to a Smaller Unit**	Example 2 **Convert to a Larger Unit**
2 km = _____ m	50 cm = _____ m
Multiply because we will need more of the smaller units.	Divide because we will need fewer of the larger units.
Convert kilometers to meters.	**Convert centimeters to meters.**
Multiply by 1,000 because 1,000 m = 1 km.	Divide by 100 because 100 cm = 1 m.
2 km = <u>2,000</u> m (2 × 1,000 = 2,000)	50 cm = <u>0.5</u> m (50 ÷ 100 = 0.5)

Complete.

1. 15 m = <u>15,000</u> mm

2. 0.36 km = <u>360</u> m

3. 2,040 mm = <u>2.04</u> m

4. 9.2 m = <u>920</u> cm

5. 877 cm = <u>8.77</u> m

6. 31 mm = <u>0.31</u> m

7. 2.39 m = <u>239</u> cm

8. 450 m = <u>0.45</u> km

9. 4,850 mm = <u>4.85</u> m

10. 57 m = <u>0.051</u> km

11. 8.6 km = <u>8600</u> m

12. 41 cm = <u>0.41</u> m

▶ Solving Problems with Hidden Information

13. Jenny knitted a scarf that was 2.6 meters long. She made an identical scarf every month for 2 years. How many centimeters of scarf had she knitted all together by the end of 2 years?

a. How many meters of scarf did Jenny knit in 1 month? **2.6**

b. For how many months did Jenny knit? **24** .

c. How many scarves did she knit during that time? _____

d. How many meters is that? _____

e. How many centimeters of scarf did Jenny knit in 2 years? _____

Solve. Check that your answer is reasonable.

Show your work.

14. Natasha ran 3.1 kilometers. Tonya ran 4 meters more than half as far as Natasha. How many meters did Tonya run?

_____

15. A European swallow flies about 11 meters in 1 second. How many kilometers could it fly in 15 minutes?

_____

16. Allie needs 65 centimeters of fabric for the pillow she is making. The fabric costs $4.20 for a meter and the stuffing for the pillow costs 79¢. How much will it cost her to make the pillow?

_____

17. Leon is building a square picture frame. The side of the frame is 345 millimeters long. If a meter of wood costs $7, how much will the wood he needs cost?

_____

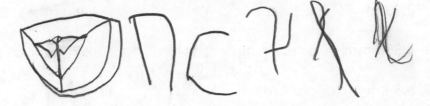

Convert Metric Units of Length

► Solving Problems with Hidden Information (continued)

Solve. Estimate to check if your answer is reasonable.   *Show your work.*

18. Pascal wants to ride his bike to and from school 3 days
    a week. His house is 2.58 kilometers from his school.
    How many meters will he ride in 7 weeks?

    _____

19. If Sabrina's hair grows 1.1 centimeters every month,
    how many meters could her hair grow over 5 years?

► What's the Error?

Dear Math Students,

I want to build a fence around my rectangular
garden. My garden is 675 centimeters long
and 225 centimeters wide. The fencing costs
$3 for every meter of fencing.

This is how I found the cost of the fencing.
Am I correct?

    6.75 m
  + 2.25 m $3 x 9 = $27
    9.00 m

Your friend,
Puzzled Penguin

20. Write a response to Puzzled Penguin.

_____

_____

_____

_____

▶ Multistep Problem Solving

Solve. Check that your answer is reasonable.

Show your work.

21. Mai has a piece of cloth that is 8.35 meters long. How many 15-centimeter pieces can she cut from the cloth? How much will be left over?

_____

22. On the first day of her 5-day trip, Miss Gordon drove 435 kilometers in 5.3 hours. On each of the next three days, she drove 80.78 kilometers in 65 minutes. On the fifth day, she drove 880 meters. How many kilometers did she drive in all?

_____

23. Paula's painting has a perimeter of 1.47 meters. She wants to put ribbon around the edge. If the ribbon comes in pieces that are 25 centimeters long, how many pieces of ribbon does she need to go all the way around her painting?

_____

24. Mattie is making a collar for her dog. She needs to buy some chain, a clasp, and a name tag. She wants the chain to be 40 centimeters long. One meter of chain costs $9.75. The clasp is $1.29 and the name tag is $3.43. How much will it cost to make the collar? Estimate to check if your answer is reasonable.

_____

Estimate: _____

25. Cam rode her bike 5 times as far as Dante did. Dante rode 187 meters farther than Michael did. Cam rode 15.25 kilometers. How many meters did Michael ride? Explain how you got your answer.

_____

_____

Convert Metric Units of Length

CA CC Content Standards **5.MD.1**
Mathematical Practices **MP.1, MP.7, MP.8**

▶ Liquid Volume

A liter is the basic unit of metric liquid volume. This chart shows the relationship between liters and other metric units of liquid volume.

Metric Units of Liquid Volume	
1 dekaliter (daL) = 10 liters	1 liter = 0.1 dekaliter
1 hectoliter (hL) = 100 liters	1 liter = 0.01 hectoliter
1 kiloliter (kL) = 1,000 liters	1 liter = 0.001 kiloliter
1 liter = 10 deciliters (dL)	0.1 liter = 1 deciliter
1 liter = 100 centiliters (cL)	0.01 liter = 1 centiliter
1 liter = 1,000 milliliters (mL)	0.001 liter = 1 milliliter

Example 1 **Convert to a Smaller Unit**	Example 2 **Convert to a Larger Unit**
5 L = _____ mL	300 mL = _____ L
Multiply because we will need more of the smaller units.	Divide because we will need fewer of the larger units.
Convert liters to milliliters.	**Convert milliliters to liters.**
Multiply by 1,000 because 1,000 L = 1 mL.	Divide by 1,000 because 1,000 mL = 1 L.
5 L = <u>5,000</u> mL (5 × 1,000 = 5,000)	300 mL = <u>0.3</u> L (300 ÷ 1,000 = 0.3)

Complete.

1. 49 L = <u>49,000</u> mL

2. 5.68 kL = <u>5,680</u> L

3. 508 mL = <u>0.508</u> L

4. 8.6 L = <u>860</u> cL

5. 483 cL = <u>4.83</u> L

6. 227 mL = <u>0.227</u> L

7. 2.9 L = <u>2,900</u> mL

8. 4,873 L = <u>4.873</u> kL

9. 1,992 mL = <u>1.992</u> L

10. 43 L = <u>0.043</u> kL

11. 41 kL = <u>41,000</u> L

12. 58 cL = <u>0.58</u> L

Name _____ **Date** _____

▶ Multistep Problem Solving

Solve. Check that your answer is reasonable.

Show your work.

13. Morgan's juice glass holds 225 milliliters. If she uses the glass to drink 8 glasses of water every day, how many liters of water does Morgan drink during a week?

_____

14. Erin's water bottle holds 665 milliliters. Dylan is carrying two water bottles. Each one holds 0.35 liters. Who is carrying more water? How much more?

_____

15. Sarita is selling lemonade in 300-milliliter bottles. She made two batches of lemonade. Each batch made 4.6 liters of lemonade. How much ~~will~~ lemonade will she have left over after filling her bottles?

0.0046 -

_____

16. Kelly is using a bucket to fill up a barrel with water from a well. The barrel holds 25.5 liters. The bucket holds 800 milliliters. The barrel already has 5.2 liters of water in it. What is the least number of buckets needed to fill the barrel?

_____

17. Tammy is making 5 batches of punch for the school's Spring Carnival. The recipe for one batch uses 1 liter of orange juice, 550 milliliters of lemon juice, 2.6 liters of soda water, and two 750 milliliter bottles of apple cider. How much punch will she make?

_____

Metric Units of Liquid Volume

▶ Convert Units of Mass

A gram is the basic unit of metric mass. This chart shows the
relationship between grams and other metric units of mass.

Metric Units of Mass	
1 dekagram (dag) = 10 grams	1 gram = 0.1 dekagram
1 hectogram (hg) = 100 grams	1 gram = 0.01 hectogram
1 kilogram (kg) = 1,000 grams	1 gram = 0.001 kilogram
1 gram = 10 decigrams (dg)	0.1 gram = 1 decigram
1 gram = 100 centigrams (cg)	0.01 gram = 1 centigram
1 gram = 1,000 milligrams (mg)	0.001 gram = 1 milligram

Example 1 Convert to a Smaller Unit

5 kg = _____ g

Multiply because we will need more
of the smaller units.

Convert kilograms to grams.

Multiply by 1,000 because 1,000 g = 1 kg.

5 kg = <u>5,000</u> g   (5 × 1,000 = 5,000)

Example 2 Convert to a Larger Unit

700 mg = _____ g

Divide because we will need fewer
of the larger units.

Convert milligrams to grams.

Divide by 1,000 because 1,000 mg = 1 g.

700 mg = <u>0.7</u> g   (700 ÷ 1,000 = 0.7)

Complete.

1. 0.003 g = _____ mg

2. 3.05 kg = _____ g

3. 25 mg = _____ g

4. 5.7 g = _____ mg

5. 294 mg = 0.294 _____

6. 0.032 g = 32 _____

7. 13.7 g = _____ mg

8. 2,441 g = _____ kg

9. 8,240 mg = _____ g

10. 75 g = 0.075 _____

11. 0.43 kg = _____ g

12. 721 mg = _____ g

▶ Multistep Problem Solving

Solve. Check that your answer is reasonable.

Show your work.

13. Hiro has 5 kilograms of potatoes and 2 kilograms of onions.
He plans to use 3.25 kilograms of potatoes and ~~550 grams~~ 0.55 kg
of onions for a recipe. How many total kilograms of the
produce will not be used?

    3.20 kg
    _____

14. A U.S. nickel has a mass of 5.00 grams. A U.S. penny has
a mass of 2.50 grams. What is the mass in kilograms of
the coins in a bag containing 186 nickels and 72 pennies?

    _____

15. Jerry is making trail mix for his camping trip. He has
200 grams of peanuts, 350 grams of raisins, and 735 grams
of pretzels. He wants to make 2 kilograms of trail mix.
How many more grams of ingredients does he need to
add to the mix?

    _____

16. Garner is helping his mom carry in the groceries. She is
carrying a bag that has a mass of 1.33 kilograms. Garner is
carrying two bags. One has a mass of 580 grams and the
other a mass of 790 grams. Who is carrying the more and
by how much?

    _____

17. Mr. Frank has 1.03 kilograms of fertilizer for the plants in
his nursery. He wants every plant to get 95 mg of fertilizer
4 times each year. What is the number of plants he could
fertilize with that amount? How much fertilizer will
he have left over?

    _____

Metric Units of Mass

Name

Date

CA CC Content Standards **5.MD.1**
Mathematical Practices **MP.1, MP.2, MP.6**

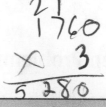

2⅟
1760
× 3
5 280

VOCABULARY
mile (mi)

▶ Convert Units

2 ⟌ 1760
-16
1 6̶ 00

Customary Units of Length

1 foot (ft) = 12 inches (in.)

1 yard (yd) = 3 feet = 36 inches

1 mile (mi) = 1,760 yards = 5,280 feet

Example 1 Convert to a Smaller Unit	**Example 2 Convert to a Larger Unit**
15 yd = _____ ft	48 in. = _____ ft
Multiply because we will need more of the smaller units.	Divide because we will need fewer of the larger units.
Convert yards to feet.	**Convert inches to feet.**
Multiply by 3 because 3 ft = 1 yd.	Divide by 12 because 12 in. = 1 ft.
15 yd = __45__ ft (15 × 3 = 45)	48 in. = __4__ ft (48 ÷ 12 = 4)

Complete.

886

1. 24 in. = __2__ ft   ↑880

1½

2. 24 ft = __8__ yd

3. 12 ft = __144__ in.   ↑1760

4. __4.5__ ft = 1½ yd

5. __18__ ft = 6 yd   1760

6. __880__ ft = ½ mi

7. __5,280__ yd = 3 mi   4.5

8. __4.5__ ft = 54 in.

9. __4__ yd = 144 in.

10. 2½ yd = __90__ in.

▶ Calculate Perimeter

Calculate the perimeter of each figure in feet.

11.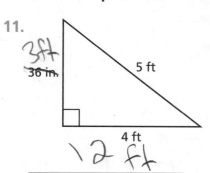
3ft
36 in.
5 ft
4 ft
12 ft

12.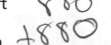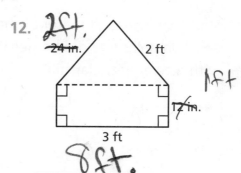
2ft.
24 in.
2 ft
1ft
12 in.
3 ft
8ft.

▶ Solve Multistep Problems

Solve. Check that your answer is reasonable.

Show your work.

13. Nick needs 65 yards of wire for a project. If the wire is only sold on spools which hold 6 feet of wire, how many spools will he need?

    33 spools

14. Jessi has 9 feet of blue fabric. To finish making her costume she needs one third of that amount of red fabric. The fabric store sells fabric by the yard. How much fabric does Jessi need to buy?

    2, 40 ~~yards~~ ✗ plus 100 yards +

15. Jay runs $1\frac{1}{2}$ miles at track practice. Teddy runs the 100-yard dash, and Cadi runs half as far as Jay. How many yards do they run all together?

    4060 yards

16. Kelly is hanging shelves in her closet. She can buy shelves for $1.25 a foot. Kelly buys one 5-foot shelf and a shelf that measures 24 inches. The rest of her materials cost $90. How much change will she get it she pays with $100?

17. Paula ran 24 ft with the football and then passed it 15 feet to Newt. Newt ran 70 yards for a touchdown. What was the total number of feet the ball traveled?

    249 feet

18. Patrick bought 54 inches of material that costs $3.40 for one yard. What change did he get if he paid for the material with a twenty-dollar bill?

    1.5

Customary Units of Length

Name _____ Date _____

CA CC Content Standards **5.MD.1**
Mathematical Practices **MP.1, MP.2, MP.6, MP.7**

▶ Fractions and Liquid Volume

In the United States we use customary units to measure.

Customary Units of Liquid Volume						
1 gallon (gal)	=	4 quarts	=	8 pints	=	16 cups (c)
$\frac{1}{4}$ gallon	=	1 quart (qt)	=	2 pints	=	4 cups
$\frac{1}{8}$ gallon	=	$\frac{1}{2}$ quart	=	1 pint (pt)	=	2 cups

Answer with a fraction in simplest form.

1. What fraction of 1 gallon is 3 quarts?

   $\frac{3}{4}$ gallon

2. What fraction of 1 quart is 1 pint?

   1/2

3. What fraction of 1 quart is 1 cup?

   1/4

4. What fraction of 1 gallon is 3 pints?

   $\frac{3}{8}$

Example 1 Convert to a Smaller Unit	**Example 2 Convert to a Larger Unit**
12 qt = _____ cups	104 pt = _____ gal
Multiply because we will need more of the smaller units.	Divide because we will need fewer of the larger units.
Convert quarts to cups.	**Convert pints to gallons.**
Multiply by 4 because 4 cups = 1 qt.	Divide by 8 because 8 pt = 1 gal.
12 qt = __48__ cups (12 × 4 = 48)	104 pt = __13__ gal (104 ÷ 8 = 13)

Complete.

5. 20 cups = __5__ qt

6. __16__ pt = 2 gal

7. 15 qt = __60__ cups

8. 3 cups = __7.5__ pt

9. __12__ gal = 48 qt

10. 144 cups = __9__ gal

11. __6__ pt = $2\frac{1}{2}$ qt

12. 23 pt = __46__ cups

13. __6__ qt = $1\frac{1}{2}$ gal

▶ Solve Multistep Problems

Solve. Check that your answer is reasonable.

Show your work.

14. A muffin recipe requires $2\frac{3}{4}$ cups of milk. What amount of milk do you need to make double the number of muffins?

   $5\frac{1}{2}$ cups

15. A recipe requires $\frac{3}{4}$ cup of water. Farha has a measuring cup that is marked only in ounces, but she knows that 8 ounces is equivalent to 1 cup. How many ounces of water will she add to the mixture? Explain.

   6

16. A serving size for pineapple-orange punch is $\frac{1}{2}$ cup. Liam needs to make 72 servings of punch. He will use 8 pints of pineapple juice. The rest is orange juice. How many pints of orange juice does he need to make the punch?

17. Melanie and Brad each drink 10 cups of water every day. Lara drinks 3 quarts of water every day. How many gallons of water do the three of them drink altogether each week?

18. Angela and Ryou are painting a room. Angela has $2\frac{1}{2}$ gallons of blue paint and Ryou has half as much white paint. It will take $2\frac{3}{4}$ quarts to cover each wall. If each wall is painted only one color, how many walls will be blue and how many will be white? How much paint will be left over?

Name _____ **Date** _____

CA CC Content Standards **5.MD.1**
Mathematical Practices **MP.1, MP.2, MP.3, MP.6, MP.7**

> **VOCABULARY**
> ton

► Fractions and Weight

Customary units of weight include ounces, pounds, and **tons**.

ounce (oz)	pound (lb)	ton (T)
1 lb = 16 oz	**1 lb**	1 T = 2,000 lb

1. The table below shows how to use fractions to compare ounces to pounds. Complete the table by writing each fraction in simplest form.

Ounces (oz)	1	2	4	8	12
Pounds (lb)	$\frac{1}{16}$	$\frac{1}{8}$	$\frac{1}{4}$	$\frac{1}{2}$	0.75

Example 1 **Convert to a Smaller Unit**	Example 2 **Convert to a Larger Unit**
4 T = _____ lb	144 oz = _____ lb
Multiply because we will need more of the smaller units.	Divide because we will need fewer of the larger units.
Convert tons to pounds.	**Convert ounces to pounds.**
Multiply by 2,000 because 2,000 lb = 1 T.	Divide by 16 because 16 oz = 1 lb.
4 T = <u>8,000</u> lb (4 × 2,000 = 8,000)	144 oz = <u>9</u> lb (144 ÷ 16 = 9)

Complete.

2. 64 oz = _____ lb

3. _____ T = 10,000 lb

4. 11 T = _____ lb

5. 16 lb = _____ oz

6. _7_ T = 14,000 lb

7. 160 oz = _____ lb

8. _____ oz = $5\frac{1}{4}$ lb

9. 848 oz = _53_ lb

10. _____ lb = 720 oz

► Solve Multistep Problems

Solve. Check that your answer is reasonable.

11. A $\frac{1}{4}$-lb package of sunflower seeds costs 79¢. An 8-ounce package costs $1.59. Which package represents the lower cost per ounce?

_____

12. Melissa is measuring 132 oz of rice into one-pound containers. How many one-pound containers will she need to hold all of the rice? How many ounces of rice will she need to buy if she needs 10 pounds of rice?

_____

13. A casserole recipe calls for 4 ounces of cheese. Adrian wants to use $\frac{1}{2}$ of the amount of cheese in his casseroles. How many pounds of cheese does he need to make 28 casseroles with his revised recipe?

_____

14. The four elephants at the Sunnypark Zoo each eat 150 pounds of food a day. The bulk of their diet is hay, but they also eat fruits, vegetables, and pellet food. How many tons of food do the four elephants eat during the month of April?

_____

15. A cargo truck is carrying three identical boxes. The weight of each box is $2\frac{1}{2}$ tons. Explain how to use mental math to find the total weight of the boxes in pounds.

_____

_____

_____

Customary Units of Weight

Name _____ **Date** _____

CA CC Content Standards 5.MD.2
Mathematical Practices MP.3, MP.4, MP.5, MP.6, MP.8

▶ Line Plots

Two number cubes, labeled 1 to 6, were tossed 30 times. This **frequency table** shows the number of times each total occurred. You can organize data on a **line plot** to make the data easier to analyze.

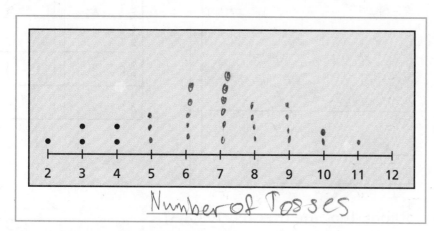

Number of Tosses

Totals for 2 cubes	Number of tosses
2	1
3	2
4	2
5	3
6	5
7	6
8	4
9	4
10	2
11	1
12	0

1. The line plot has been filled in for tosses of 2, 3, and 4. Complete the rest of the line plot.

2. Based on this sample, describe the totals that are least likely to be tossed.

   12, 11, 2, 10, 4, 3, 5

3. Based on this sample, describe the totals that are most likely to be tossed.

   6, 7, 8, 9, ~~8~~

4. Why doesn't a total of 1 appear on the line plot or in the table?

   Because, the lowest total you can roll on the dice is 2, there is no zero

5. Explain why a total of 7 was the most likely sum tossed.

   _____
   _____
   _____

► Line Plots with Fractional Units

6. For 10 days, Mario measured the amount of food that his cat Toby ate each day. The amounts he recorded are shown in the table at the right. Graph the results on the line plot.

Amounts Toby Ate Each Day for 10 Days	
$\frac{1}{4}$ c	||
$\frac{3}{8}$ c	|
$\frac{1}{2}$ c	|||
$\frac{5}{8}$ c	|||
$\frac{3}{4}$ c	|

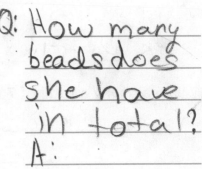

Amounts Toby Ate Each Day for 10days

a. What is the total amount of food Toby ate over the 10 days? Explain how you got your answer.

5.25 cups / 5$\frac{1}{4}$ cups

b. What amount of food would Toby get if the total for 10 days was distributed evenly each day?

7. Lilly bought a bag of beads of mixed sizes. She made the frequency table below showing the number of beads of each size. Make a line plot using her data. Write a question that can be solved using the line plot.

Diameter of Beads (in.)	
$\frac{1}{8}$	|||||
$\frac{1}{4}$	|||
$\frac{3}{8}$	||||
$\frac{1}{2}$	||

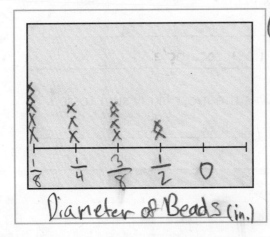

Diameter of Beads (in.)

Q: How many beads does she have in total?
A:

Read and Make Line Plots

Name _____ **Date** _____

CA CC Content Standards 5.NF.4b
Mathematical Practices MP.3, MP.6, MP.8

► Discuss Perimeter and Area

Perimeter is the distance around a figure.

Rectangle A

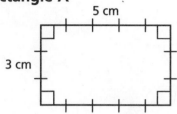

5 cm

3 cm

$P = 3$ cm $+ 5$ cm $+ 3$ cm $+ 5$ cm $= 16$ cm

Formula: $2(l + w)$

Area is the total number of square units that cover a figure.

$5 \times \frac{x}{8} + \frac{x}{5} = \frac{8}{15}$

Rectangle B

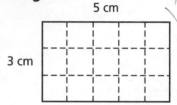

5 cm

3 cm

$A = 3$ cm $\times 5$ cm $= 15$ sq cm

Formula: 53

► Discuss Fractional Side Lengths

To find the area of a rectangle with fractional side lengths, use the same method you use to find the area of a rectangle with whole-number side lengths.

Rectangle C

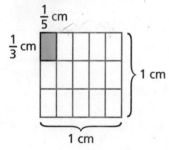

$\frac{1}{5}$ cm

$\frac{1}{3}$ cm

1 cm

1 cm

$A = 1$ of 15 equal parts

$A = \frac{1}{3}$ cm $\times \frac{1}{5}$ cm $= \frac{1}{15}$ sq cm

Rectangle D

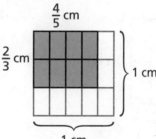

$\frac{4}{5}$ cm

$\frac{2}{3}$ cm

1 cm

1 cm

$A =$ eight $\frac{1}{15}$'s

$A = \frac{2}{3}$ cm $\times \frac{4}{5}$ cm $= \frac{8}{15}$ sq cm

Find the perimeter of each green rectangle.

1. Rectangle C: _____

2. Rectangle D: _____

3. Discuss how finding the perimeter of a rectangle with fractional side lengths is the same as and different from finding the perimeter of a rectangle with whole-number side lengths.

▶ Analyze Area Models with Fractional Side Lengths

Solve.

4. Shade and label the model to show the area of a $\frac{1}{2}$ mi by $\frac{1}{4}$ mi rectangle. Describe what your model shows and then find the area numerically.

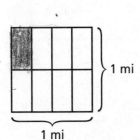

$\frac{1}{8}$ mi

_____

_____

_____

_____

5. Shade the model to show the area of a $\frac{1}{2}$ mi by $\frac{3}{4}$ mi rectangle. Describe what your model shows and then find the area numerically.

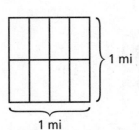

$\frac{3}{8}$ mi

_____

_____

_____

▶ Find an Unknown Side Length

6. What is the length of a rectangle with a width of 27 feet and an area of 918 square feet?

34 feet

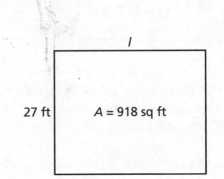

27 ft $A = 918$ sq ft

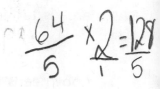

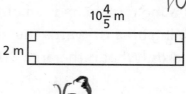

▶ Practice with Area

Find the perimeter and the area of the rectangle.

7.
$\frac{1}{2}$ cm
$\frac{1}{2}$ cm

$\frac{1}{2}$

P = 2

A = $\frac{1}{4}$

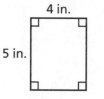

8.
$10\frac{4}{5}$ m
2 m

P = $25\frac{3}{5}$

A = _____

$12\frac{4}{5}$

9.
4 in.
5 in.

P = _____

A = _____

10.
$1\frac{4}{5}$ cm
$\frac{2}{3}$ cm

$\frac{64}{5} \times \frac{2}{1} = \frac{128}{5}$

P = _____

A = $\frac{128}{5}$

Find the side length of the rectangle.

11.
_____ m
4.8 m   A = 29.76 sq m

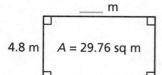

12.
$\frac{1}{3}$ ft
_____ ft   A = 2 sq ft

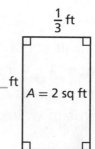

13.
_____ cm
5.6 cm   A = 62.72 sq cm

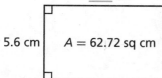

14.
$3\frac{1}{2}$ yd
$\frac{1}{2}$ yd   A = 7 sq yd

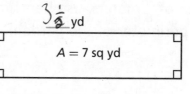

Name _____ Date _____

▶ Solve Real World Problems

Solve.

15. Brian was tiling a patio and ran out of tiles. The width of the remaining area is $\frac{2}{3}$ yard. The length of the remaining area is 4 yards. What is the area Brian has left to tile?

_____

16. Rylee knows that the area for the face-painting station is 166 square feet. She knows that the length of the rectangular area is 12 feet. How wide is the area?

1992
_____

17. Coby needs to know the area and perimeter of his farm property. The length of his property is $\frac{1}{12}$ mile and the width is $\frac{3}{8}$ mile. What is the area? What is the perimeter?

$\frac{1}{32}$ mile $\frac{11}{12}$ mile
_____

18. The area for the dance floor is 45 square feet, and one side is 8 feet. What is the length of the other side?

_____

19. Margo wants new carpet and a new wallpaper border for her bedroom. The room is 5.4 meters long and $4\frac{7}{8}$ meters wide. About how many square yards of carpet will she need? About how many yards of wallpaper border will she need?

_____

20. Tomas has a garden with a length of 2.45 meters and a width of $\frac{5}{8}$ meters. Use benchmarks to estimate the area and perimeter of the garden.

_____

21. Laura has a rectangular piece of wood that is 7 inches by 4 inches. She wants to cover it with strips of ribbon that are $\frac{1}{4}$ inch wide. What length of ribbon does she need to cover the wood?

Perimeter and Area of Rectangles

Name _____ **Date** _____

CA CC Content Standards 5.MD.3a, 5.MD.3b, 5.MD.4
Mathematical Practices MP.3, MP.4, MP.5, MP.6, MP.7

VOCABULARY
face
edge
unit cube
volume
cubic unit

► Describe a Cube

Use the cube to answer the questions below.

1. How many **faces** does a cube have? _____

2. How many **edges** does a cube have? _____

Write *true* or *false* for each statement.

3. All the edges of a cube are the same length. _____

4. All the faces of a cube are the same size squares. _____

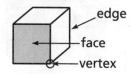

► Explore Volume

A **unit cube** is a cube with each edge 1 unit long. The volume of a unit cube is 1 **cubic unit**. The **volume** of an object can be measured by filling it with unit cubes without any gaps or overlaps.

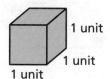

Cut out the nets. Fold each of the nets to make an open-ended prism. Fill the prisms with 1-cm cubes leaving no spaces.

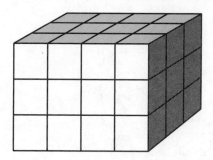

5. Number of cubes: _____

6. Volume: _____

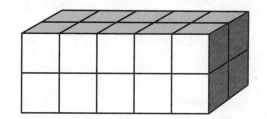

7. Number of cubes: _____

8. Volume: _____

Name _____   Date _____

▶ Unit Cubes and Volume

Find the number of unit cubes and the volume.

9.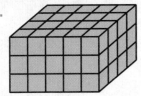

Number of unit cubes: _____

Volume: _____

10.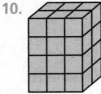

Number of cubes: _____

Volume: _____

11.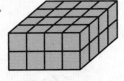

86

Number of unit cubes: _____

Volume: _____

12.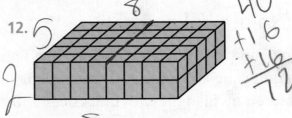

*5 8 40
    +16
2   +16
    72*

Number of unit cubes: _____

Volume: _____

▶ What's the Error?

Dear Math Students,

This drawing of a cube appears to have a volume of 19 cubic units but, when I built it, I used 27 cubes. What did I do wrong?

Your Friend,
Puzzled Penguin

13. Write a response to Puzzled Penguin.

_____

_____

_____

Cubic Units and Volume

Name _____ Date _____

▶ Nets for Rectangular Prisms

Cut out the nets and form the open-ended prism.

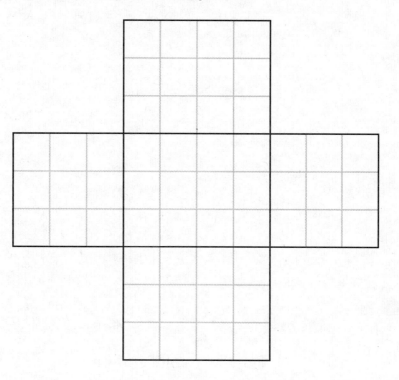

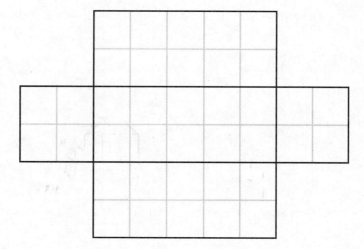

▶ Nets for Rectangular Prisms (continued)

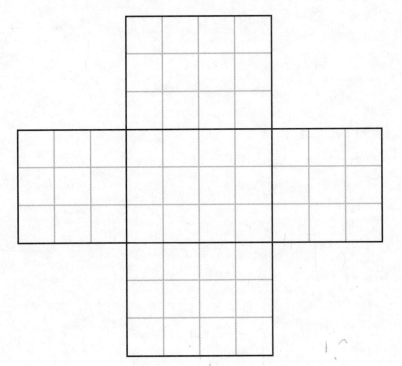

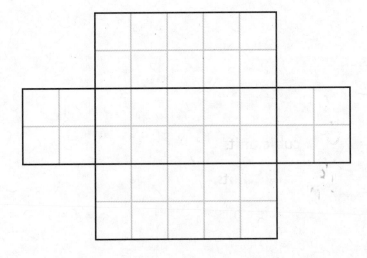

Cubic Units and Volume

Name _____ **Date** _____

CA CC Content Standards **5.MD.3, 5.MD.3a, 5.MD.3b**
Mathematical Practices **MP.2, MP.4, MP.6**

VOCABULARY
rectangular prism
volume
cubic unit

▶ Explore Layers

You can use layers of cubes to build **rectangular prisms**.

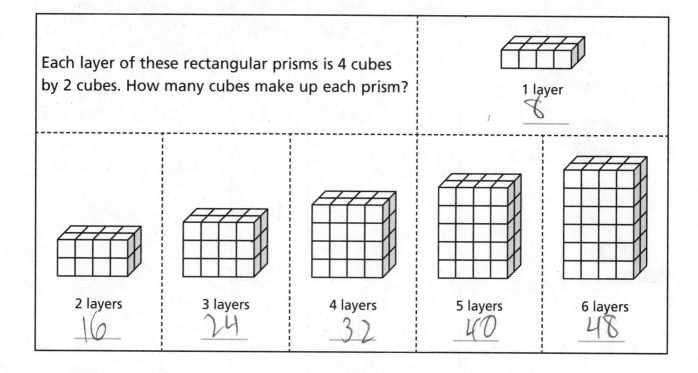

Each layer of these rectangular prisms is 4 cubes by 2 cubes. How many cubes make up each prism?

1 layer
8

2 layers
16

3 layers
24

4 layers
32

5 layers
40

6 layers
48

The **volume** of a prism is the number of cubes needed to build the prism. Volume is recorded in **cubic units**.

Write the volume of the prism in cubic units.

1. 1 layer: $4 \times 2 \times 1 =$ ___8___ cubic units

2. 2 layers: $4 \times 2 \times 2 =$ ___16___ cubic units

3. 3 layers: $4 \times 2 \times 3 =$ ___24___ cubic units

4. 4 layers: $4 \times 2 \times 4 =$ ___32___ cubic units

5. 5 layers: $4 \times 2 \times 5 =$ ___40___ cubic units

6. 6 layers: $4 \times 2 \times 6 =$ ___48___ cubic units

Name _____   Date _____

3
48
× 4
192
19

► Calculate Volume

Complete the table.

Prism	length (l)	width (w)	height (h)	(length × width) × height (l × w) × h	volume (V)
7.	7 ft	4 ft	5 ft	(7 × 4) × 5	140 cu ft
8.	6cm	15cm	10cm	(6×15)×10	900
9.	12 cm	4 cm	4 cm	(12cm×4)×4	192
10.	5 in	4 in	8 in	(5×4)×8	160
11.	15cm	10cm	7 cm	(15×10)×7	216
12.	6 in	6 in	6 in	(6×6)×6	216

Visualize Volume

Name _____ **Date** _____

CA CC Content Standards **5.MD.5a, 5.MD.5b**
Mathematical Practices **MP.1, MP.3, MP.6**

▶ Develop a Formula

1. What is the volume of this rectangular prism?

   36 cubic units

2. How do you find the area of a rectangle?

   length x width

3. How do you find the volume of a rectangular prism?

   length x width x height

4. How is finding volume different from finding area?

   _____

5. Write a formula for finding the volume of any rectangular prism.

   Volume = _____

6. This ice cube is shaped like a cube. Its edge lengths are 2 cm. What is the volume of this ice cube? Write a formula for finding the volume of any cube.

   _____

   _____

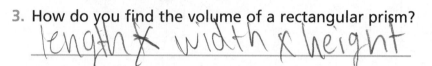

3 x 4 x 3

▶ Find an Unknown Edge

7. Raul is building a planter in the shape of a rectangular prism. It has a length of 4 feet and a height of 2 feet. How wide should it be to hold 24 cubic feet of soil? Explain how you found your answer.

   _____

   _____

   _____

   _____

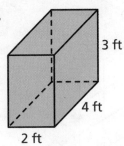

► Practice

Write a numerical expression for the volume. Then calculate the volume.

8.

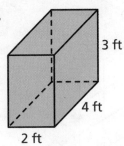

3 ft
4 ft
2 ft

Expression: _____

Volume: _____

9.

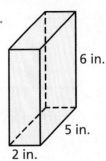

6 in.
5 in.
2 in.

Expression: _____

Volume: _____

10.

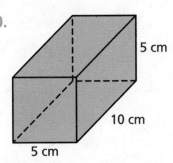

5 cm
10 cm
5 cm

Expression: _____

Volume: _____

Find the unknown dimension or volume of each rectangular prism.

11. $V = 120$ cu m

$l = 4$ m

$w = $ _____

$h = 5$ m

12. $V = 120$ cu in.

$l = $ _____

$w = 4$ in.

$h = 3$ in.

13. $V = $ _____

$l = 7$ cm

$w = 6$ cm

$h = 7$ cm

Write an equation. Then solve.

14. A box shaped like a rectangular prism is 2 m long, 2 m wide, and has a height of 3 m. What is the volume of the box?

_____

15. Fred's dog crate is 42 inches long, 24 inches wide, and has a height of 30 inches. What is the volume of the crate?

_____

16. The cargo hold of a truck has a height of 3 yards and is 5 yards wide. The volume of the cargo hold is listed as 240 cubic yards. What is the length of the cargo hold?

_____

Introduce Volume Formulas

© Houghton Mifflin Harcourt Publishing Company

Name _____   **Date** _____

CA CC Content Standards **5.MD.5b**
Mathematical Practices **MP.6**

▶ Compare Length, Area, and Volume

Length tells how wide, tall, or long something is.
Finding length requires one measurement.
Length is **one-dimensional** and is measured in
linear units.

Area tells how much surface a figure covers.
Finding the area of a rectangle requires two linear
measurements. Area is **two-dimensional** and is
measured in square units.

Volume tells how much space an object occupies.
Finding the volume of a rectangular prism requires three
linear measurements. Volume is **three-dimensional** and
is measured in cubic units.

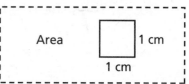

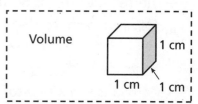

To answer the question, tell if you need to measure for length, area, or volume. Then write the number of measurements you need to make.

1. How much water is in a swimming pool? _volume 3_

2. How tall are you? _length 1_

3. How much carpet is needed for a floor? _area 2_

4. How far is it from a doorknob to the floor? _length 1_

5. How much sand is in a sandbox? _volume 3_

6. How much wallpaper is needed for one wall? _area 2_

7. How long is a string? _length 1_

8. How much space is there inside a refrigerator? _area ~~3~~ 2_

▶ Solve Real World Problems

Solve.

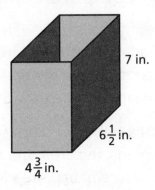

7 in.

$6\frac{1}{2}$ in.

$4\frac{3}{4}$ in.

9. Soledad has a storage box. The box is $6\frac{1}{2}$ inches long, $4\frac{3}{4}$ inches wide, and 7 inches tall. She wants to run a border around the top of the box. How much border does she need ?

_____

10. The refrigerator is $5\frac{2}{3}$ feet tall, $2\frac{2}{7}$ feet wide, and $2\frac{1}{4}$ feet deep. How much space does the refrigerator take up on the floor?

_____

11. Melissa is stacking storage cubes in a crate. The bottom of the crate is 8 inches by 12 inches. The volume of the crate is 768 cu inches. If a storage cube has a length of 4 inches, how many storage cubes will fit in the crate?

_____

12. Reed has a lawn mowing service and charges $1.00 for mowing 15 square yards of lawn. On Saturday he mows 5 lawns that are each $21\frac{3}{4}$ yards by 27 yards. How much money does Reed earn on Saturday?

_____

13. Parker builds a planter in the shape of a rectangular prism that is 6 feet wide, 3 feet deep, and 2 feet tall. How much soil will he need to fill it?

_____

14. A box is a rectangular prism with a square base. The volume is 972 cubic centimeters and the area of the square base is 81 square centimeters. What is the height of the box? Explain how you found your answer.

_____

8-13

Class Activity

Name _____

Date _____

CA CC Content Standards 5.MD.5. 5.MD.5b, 5.MD.5c
Mathematical Practices MP.1, MP.6, MP.8

▶ Analyze a Composite Solid Figure

A **composite** solid can be made by putting together
two or more rectangular prisms. To find the volume
of such a composite solid, divide it into individual
prisms. Use the formula $V = l \cdot w \cdot h$ to find the
volume of each individual prism, and then add
the volumes to find the total volume.

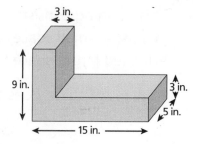

**To find the volume, you can decompose the solid into
different rectangular prisms.**

1. Find the volume of the blue rectangular prism first.

$V = \underline{9} \times \underline{3} \times \underline{5} = \underline{135}$ cubic inches

$V = \underline{15} \times \underline{3} \times \underline{5} = \underline{225}$ cubic inches

Total volume = $\underline{135} + \underline{225} = \underline{360}$ cubic inches

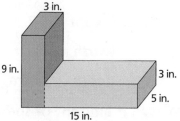

2. Find the volume of the blue rectangular prism first.

$V = \underline{15} \times \underline{3} \times \underline{5} = \underline{225}$ cubic inches

$V = \underline{9} \times \underline{3} \times \underline{5} = \underline{135}$ cubic inches

Total volume = $\underline{225} + \underline{135} = \underline{360}$ cubic inches

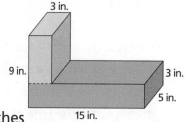

3. **Discuss** Compare your answers to Problems 1 and 2.
What conclusion or conclusions can you make?

$5 \times 2 \times 4 = 40$

▶ Practice

Find the volume of each composite solid figure.

$\frac{\times 12}{72}$

4.

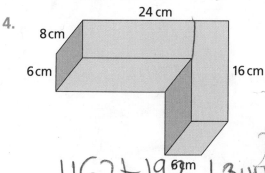

$6 \times$

$\begin{array}{r} 12 \\ \times 10 \\ \hline \end{array}$ $120 +$

$V = \underline{1152 + 192 = 1,344}$

cubic
cm

$\frac{+72}{192}$

5.

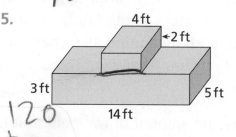

$V = \underline{210 + 40 = 250 \, ft}$

© Houghton Mifflin Harcourt Publishing Company

Name _1,188 / 160_ _+_ **Date** _18000 + 750 = 18750_

▶ Real World Problems

6. This building consists of two rectangular prisms—a small space for offices and an attached larger space for warehouse storage.

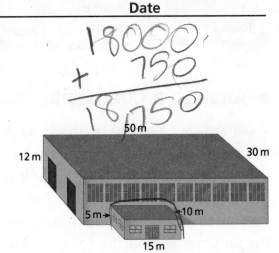

How much space does the building take up?

18,750 cubic m

7. When Jayna's notebook computer is open, it has the following dimensions:

top *height* = 0.7 cm   **bottom** *height* = 1.5 cm

width = 33 cm   *width* = 33 cm

depth = 24 cm   *depth* = 24 cm

What amount of space does Jayna's notebook take up when it is closed?

1742.4 cubic cm

8. The size of a furnace depends on the volume of air in a building. A heating contractor must size a furnace for the three-unit apartment building shown in the sketch at the right.

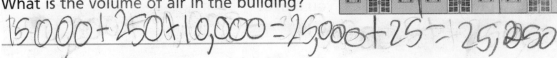

What is the volume of air in the building?

_15000 + 250 + 10,000 = 25,000 + 25 = 25,250_

9. An in-ground swimming pool often has steps that are made from poured concrete. In the sketch of the steps at the right, the steps are identical, each measuring 18 inches from side to side, 12 inches from front to back, and 8 inches tall.

Calculate the amount of concrete that is needed to form the steps.

1728 cubic in.

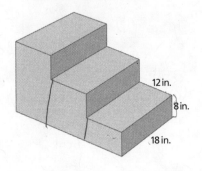

Volume of Composite Solid Figures

► Reasoning About Quadrilaterals

In Exercises 1–6, write *true* or *false*. If the statement is false, sketch a counterexample.

1. All quadrilaterals have at least one pair of parallel sides.

   true

2. All squares have a pair of perpendicular sides.

   false   ▯

3. A rhombus must have an acute angle.

   false   ◇

4. All rectangles have opposite sides that are the same length.

   true

5. All squares have opposite sides that are parallel.

   true

6. A quadrilateral with a right angle must be a rectangle.

   false

Sketch a shape that fits the description if possible.

7. a parallelogram with exactly two right angles

8. a trapezoid with one line of symmetry

9. a rectangle with adjacent sides that are the same length

10. a square that is not a rhombus

© Houghton Mifflin Harcourt Publishing Company

VOCABULARY
quadrilateral
parallelogram
trapezoid
rectangle
rhombus
square

▶ Classify Quadrilaterals

A **quadrilateral** is a closed shape with four straight sides.
The diagram below shows how the categories of quadrilaterals
are related.

11. List the letters of the shapes from Quadrilaterals A–T
   that belong in each category. (Many shapes belong to
   more than one category.) Then complete the statements.

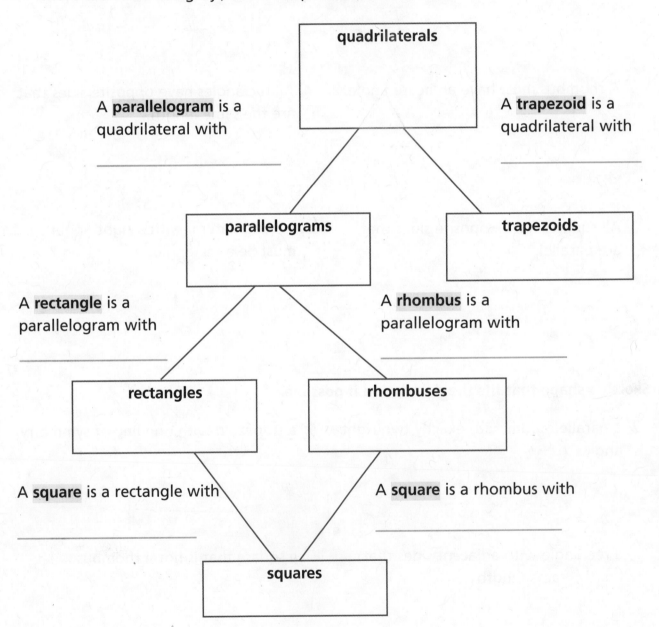

A **parallelogram** is a
quadrilateral with

_____

A **trapezoid** is a
quadrilateral with

_____

A **rectangle** is a
parallelogram with

_____

A **rhombus** is a
parallelogram with

_____

A **square** is a rectangle with

_____

A **square** is a rhombus with

_____

Attributes of Quadrilaterals

► Quadrilateral Cards

quadrilateral A	quadrilateral B	quadrilateral C	quadrilateral D
quadrilateral E	quadrilateral F	quadrilateral G	quadrilateral H
quadrilateral I	quadrilateral J	quadrilateral K	quadrilateral L
quadrilateral M	quadrilateral N	quadrilateral O	quadrilateral P
quadrilateral Q	quadrilateral R	quadrilateral S	quadrilateral T

8-15
Class Activity

Name _____

Date _____

CA CC Content Standards 5.G.3, 5.G.4
Mathematical Practices MP.1, MP.4, MP.5, MP.6, MP.7

▶ Reasoning About Triangles

In Exercises 1–6, write *true* or *false*. If the statement is false, sketch a counterexample.

1. All isosceles triangles are also equilateral.

2. A scalene triangle cannot have a line of symmetry.

3. All right triangles have two acute angles.

4. Any triangle with an obtuse angle must be scalene.

5. All equilateral triangles are acute.

6. A scalene triangle cannot have a right angle.

Sketch a shape that fits the description if possible.

7. an isosceles triangle with a right angle

8. a triangle with two right angles

9. a triangle with more than one line of symmetry

10. an isosceles triangle without a line of symmetry

VOCABULARY
acute triangle
obtuse triangle
right triangle
equilateral triangle
isosceles triangle
scalene triangle

▶ Classify Triangles

Write the letters of the shapes from Triangles A–L in the
correct region of each diagram.

11.

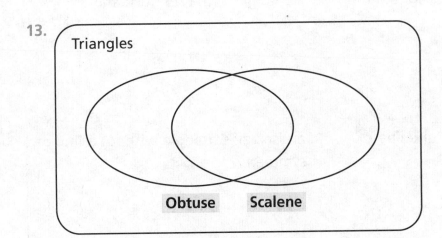

Triangles

B   L   E   C
           A   H

Right   Isosceles

12.

Triangles

C   J   J
G
L

Acute   Equilateral

13.

Triangles

Obtuse   Scalene

Attributes of Triangles

► Triangle Cards

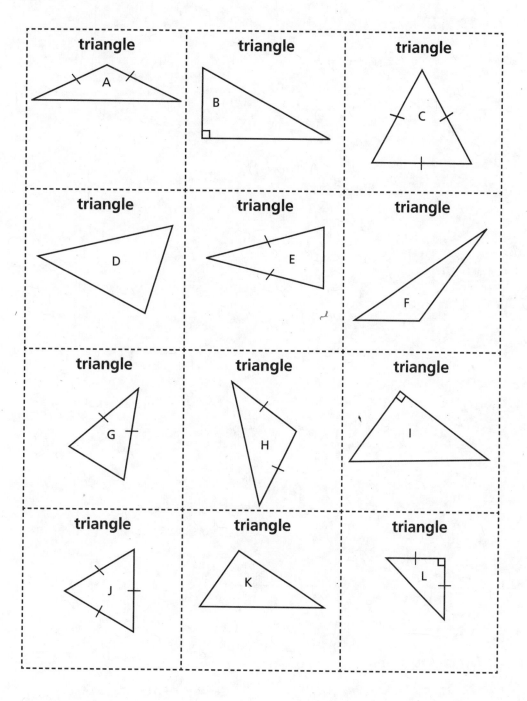

Attributes of Triangles

Name _____

Date _____

CA CC Content Standards 5.G.3, 5.G.4
Mathematical Practices MP.5, MP.6, MP.7

VOCABULARY
open   concave
closed   convex
polygon

▶ Two-Dimensional Shapes

Two-dimensional shapes can be made up of line segments or curves or both.

Two-dimensional shapes can be **open** or **closed**.

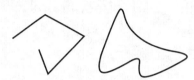

A **polygon** is a closed two-dimensional shape made from line segments that don't cross each other.

polygons   **not polygons**

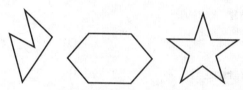

A polygon is **concave** if you can connect two points inside the polygon with a line segment that passes outside the polygon. A **convex** polygon has no such line segment. All the inside angles of a convex polygon are less than 180°.

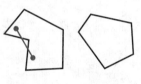

concave   convex

Tell whether each figure is a polygon. If it is not a polygon, explain why it does not fit the definition.

1.

_____

2.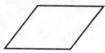

_____

3.

_____

4.

_____

5.

_____

6.

_____

VOCABULARY
regular polygon

▶ Names of Polygons

Polygons are named by the number of sides they have.
Here are some polygons with their names.

triangle	quadrilateral	pentagon	hexagon	octagon
3 sides	4 sides	5 sides	6 sides	8 sides

Polygons in which all sides are congruent *and* all angles are
congruent are called **regular polygons**. The octagon above
is a regular octagon.

Name the polygon. Then circle the terms that describe it.

7. 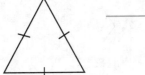 _____

regular   not regular

concave   convex

8. 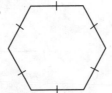 _____

regular   not regular

concave   convex

9. 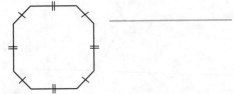 _____

regular   not regular

concave   convex

10. 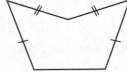 _____

regular   not regular

concave   convex

Write *true* or *false*.

11. A square is a regular quadrilateral. _____

12. It is possible to draw a concave triangle. _____

Attributes of Two-Dimensional Shapes

Name

Date

► Two-Dimensional Shape Cards

2-D shape	2-D shape	2-D shape	2-D shape
A	B	C	D
2-D shape	2-D shape	2-D shape	2-D shape
E	F	G	H
2-D shape	2-D shape	2-D shape	2-D shape
I	J	K	L
2-D shape	2-D shape	2-D shape	2-D shape
M	N	O	P

Attributes of Two-Dimensional Shapes

Name _____ Date _____

► **Attribute Cards**

concave polygon	convex polygon	straight sides	curved
open	closed	polygon	regular polygon
at least one pair of parallel sides	at least one pair of perpendicular sides	line of symmetry	at least two congruent sides
acute angle	right angle	obtuse angle	angle greater than 180°

Attributes of Two-Dimensional Shapes

Name _____ **Date** _____

CA CC Content Standards **5.MD.3, 5.MD.5, 5.MD.5b**
Mathematical Practices **MP.1, MP.2, MP.4, MP.7**

► Math and Aquariums

A goldfish bowl is a small aquarium. Other aquariums, like those found in museums, can be enormous and have computer monitored and controlled life-support systems.

Many home aquariums are made of glass or acrylic, and are shaped like rectangular prisms. A sketch of Naomi's home aquarium is shown the right.

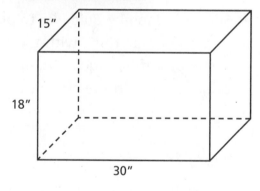

Use the sketch to solve Problems 1 and 2.

1. Which faces of Naomi's aquarium—the top and bottom, the sides, or the front and back—have the greatest perimeter?

   _____

2. Use a formula and find the area of each of the following faces.

   top and bottom _____

   left side and right side _____

   front and back _____

3. Use a formula and find the volume of the aquarium.

   _____

► Math and Aquariums (continued)

Residents of salt water aquariums often include colorful fish. Some salt water aquariums also include living plants, rocks, and corals.

Use the sketch of Naomi's aquarium shown below to solve Problems 4–6.

4. Suppose three inches of sand were placed in the bottom of the aquarium. Calculate the remaining volume of the aquarium.

5. Naomi would like to attach rubber edging along the top edges, and along the bottom edges, of her aquarium. Use a formula to determine the minimum length of edging Naomi would need.

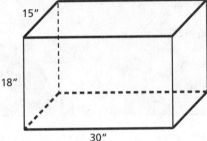

6. Suppose Naomi would like to place a flat sheet of acrylic under her aquarium, with the sheet extending 1-inch beyond the edges of her aquarium in all directions. What size sheet of acrylic should she purchase?

Solve.

7. Explain how you could change your answers to Problem 2 to square feet, and your answer to Problem 3 to cubic feet.

1. Select the length that is equivalent to 0.14 meter. Mark all that apply.

   (A) 140 kilometers   (D) 0.0014 hectometer
   (B) 0.014 millimeter   (E) 0.014 dekameter
   (C) 14 centimeters   (F) 14,000 decimeters

2. Julian is making barbecue sauce that he will put into jars. He uses 15 cups of tomato sauce, 6 cups of white vinegar, $\frac{1}{2}$ cup of honey, and $\frac{1}{2}$ cup of maple syrup. How many quart jars can he fill? How many pint jars can he fill with any leftover sauce?

   _____ quart jar(s) with _____ pint jar(s) leftover

3. The mass of a science textbook is 1.15 kilograms. The mass of a history textbook is 950 grams. Rami makes a stack of 4 science textbooks and a stack of 5 history textbooks.

   Part A

   Write <or> to compare the masses of the stacks of textbooks.

   History textbooks ◯ Science textbooks

   Part B

   By how much mass do the stacks of textbooks differ? Write your answer in kilograms. Explain how you found the difference.

4. For numbers 4a–4c, complete the conversion shown.

   4a. 1,200 mL = _____ L

   4b. _____ L = 6,000 mL

   4c. _____ mg = 0.18 g

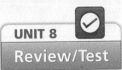

Name _____ **Date** _____

5. Write the letter for each measurement in the first column next to the equivalent measurement in the second column.

A 54 in.   [   ] 500 lb

B $10\frac{3}{4}$ lb   [   ] $4\frac{1}{2}$ ft

C 21 gal   [   ] 172 oz

D 15 yd   [   ] 24 c

E $1\frac{1}{2}$ gal   [   ] 540 in.

F $\frac{1}{4}$ ton   [   ] 84 qt

6. Use a formula and calculate the volume of the figure.

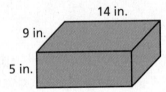

14 in.
9 in.
5 in.

[   ]

7. Write the missing dimensions of the figure. Then use a formula and calculate the volume of the figure.

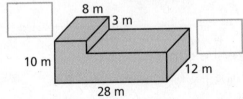

8 m
3 m
10 m
12 m
28 m

[   ]

8. For numbers 8a–8f, choose Yes or No to indicate whether the name applies to the polygon.

8a. quadrilateral   ○ Yes   ○ No

8b. rectangle   ○ Yes   ○ No

8c. square   ○ Yes   ○ No

8d. parallelogram   ○ Yes   ○ No

8e. rhombus   ○ Yes   ○ No

8f. trapezoid   ○ Yes   ○ No

9. Draw an isosceles triangle with a right angle.

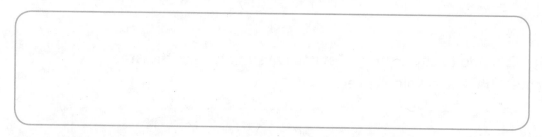

10. A path is 0.75 meter wide. Mr. Kassel extends the width by placing blocks 20 centimeters wide on each side of the path. The new path is how many meters wide?

_____ meters

11. The east side of Mrs. Hammond's ranch is 475 meters longer than the west side. The west side is 2.6 kilometers long. The east side is how many kilometers long?

_____ kilometers

12. On a 1-mile walking tour of New York City, a group had to take a detour that was 100 yards shorter than half the distance of the tour. The detour is how many yards long?

_____ yards

13. Choose a number from the first column and a unit from the second column to make a measurement that is equivalent to 240 centigrams.

Number	Unit
○ 24	○ milligrams
○ 0.024	○ decigrams
○ 2,400	○ kilograms

14. A rectangular cedar chest measures 40 inches long by 22 inches wide by 20 inches high.

Part A
Find the volume of the chest.

Part B
A cushion is made to cover the top of the chest. Calculate the area of the chest that the cushion covers.

Part C
Explain any difference in the units for the volume and the area.

15. A door sign has a length of 5 inches and an area of $8\frac{1}{8}$ square inches. Use the numbers and symbols to write an equation that can be used to find the unknown width (w). Then solve.

$w =$ _____ inches

16. A souvenir postcard is $5\frac{1}{4}$ inches long and $3\frac{1}{2}$ inches wide. What is the area of the postcard?

17. Classify the figure using the terms in the boxes. Write the letter of the figure in the correct box. A figure may be classified using more than one term.

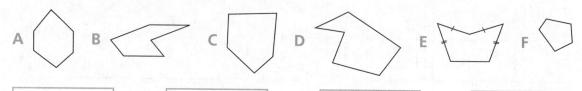

Concave	Convex	Hexagon	Pentagon

18. Bakari builds a rectangular prism using unit cubes.

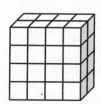

What is the volume of the prism? Explain your thinking.

19. For numbers 19a–19f, select True or False for each statement.

19a. A circle is a convex polygon.   ○ True   ○ False

19b. A rhombus can have only one right angle.   ○ True   ○ False

19c. All squares are rectangles.   ○ True   ○ False

19d. A regular octagon can be concave.   ○ True   ○ False

19e. A triangle can have at most one right angle.   ○ True   ○ False

19f. A regular triangle has three 60° angles.   ○ True   ○ False

Name _____   Date _____

20. Mika records the number of miles she walks each day.

   Part A

   Graph Mika's results on the line plot.

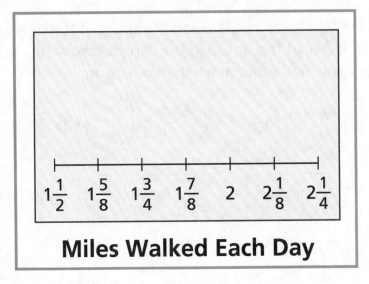

Distance (miles)	Days
$1\frac{1}{2}$	ⵌ
$1\frac{5}{8}$	I
$1\frac{3}{4}$	II
2	I
$2\frac{1}{8}$	III
$2\frac{1}{4}$	IIII

Miles Walked Each Day

   Part B

   How many days did she walk and what was her total distance? Explain your thinking.

   [   ]

Choose the term from the box to complete the statement.

21. Every rectangle is also a ⟨ parallelogram / square / rhombus ⟩ .

22. A trapezoid is also a ⟨ parallelogram / rhombus / quadrilateral ⟩ .

Reference Tables

Table of Measures

Metric	Customary

Length/Area/Volume

Metric	Customary
1 millimeter (mm) = 0.001 meter (m)	1 foot (ft) = 12 inches (in.)
1 centimeter (cm) = 0.01 meter	1 yard (yd) = 36 inches
1 decimeter (dm) = 0.1 meter	1 yard = 3 feet
1 dekameter (dam) = 10 meters	1 mile (mi) = 5,280 feet
1 hectometer (hm) = 100 meters	1 mile = 1,760 yards
1 kilometer (km) = 1,000 meters	1 acre = 4,840 square yards
1 hectare (ha) = 1,000 square meters (m²)	1 acre = 43,560 square feet
1 square centimeter = 1 sq cm	1 acre = $\frac{1}{640}$ square mile
A metric unit for measuring area. It is the area of a square that is 1 centimeter on each side.	1 square inch = 1 sq in.
	A customary unit for measuring area. It is the area of a square that is 1 inch on each side.
1 cubic centimeter = 1 cu cm	1 cubic inch = 1 cu in.
A unit for measuring volume. It is the volume of a cube with each edge 1 centimeter long.	A unit for measuring volume. It is the volume of a cube with each edge 1 inch long.

Capacity

Metric	Customary
1 milliliter (mL) = 0.001 liter (L)	1 teaspoon (tsp) = $\frac{1}{6}$ fluid ounce (fl oz)
1 centiliter (cL) = 0.01 liter	1 tablespoon (tbsp) = $\frac{1}{2}$ fluid ounce
1 deciliter (dL) = 0.1 liter	1 cup (c) = 8 fluid ounces
1 dekaliter (daL) = 10 liters	1 pint (pt) = 2 cups
1 hectoliter (hL) = 100 liters	1 quart (qt) = 2 pints
1 kiloliter (kL) = 1,000 liters	1 gallon (gal) = 4 quarts

Mass / Weight

Mass	Weight
1 milligram (mg) = 0.001 gram (g)	1 pound (lb) = 16 ounces
1 centigram (cg) = 0.01 gram	1 ton (T) = 2,000 pounds
1 decigram (dg) = 0.1 gram	
1 dekagram (dag) = 10 grams	
1 hectogram (hg) = 100 grams	
1 kilogram (kg) = 1,000 grams	
1 metric ton = 1,000 kilograms	

Volume/Capacity/Mass for Water

1 cubic centimeter = 1 milliliter = 1 gram

1,000 cubic centimeters = 1 liter = 1 kilogram

Reference Tables (continued)

Table of Units of Time

Time

1 minute (min) = 60 seconds (sec)

1 hour (hr) = 60 minutes

1 day = 24 hours

1 week (wk) = 7 days

1 month is about 30 days

1 year (yr) = 12 months (mo)
or about 52 weeks

1 year = 365 days

1 leap year = 366 days

1 decade = 10 years

1 century = 100 years

1 millennium = 1,000 years

Table of Formulas

Perimeter

Polygon $P = $ sum of the lengths of the sides

Rectangle $P = 2(l + w)$ or $P = 2l + 2w$

Square $P = 4s$

Area

Rectangle $A = l \cdot w$

Square $A = s \cdot s$ or $A = s^2$

Volume of a Rectangular Prism

$V = lwh$ or $V = Bh$

(where B is the area of the base of the prism)

Properties of Operations

Associative Property of Addition

$(a + b) + c = a + (b + c)$ $(2 + 5) + 3 = 2 + (5 + 3)$

Commutative Property of Addition

$a + b = b + a$ $4 + 6 = 6 + 4$

Additive Identity Property of 0

$a + 0 = 0 + a = a$ $3 + 0 = 0 + 3 = 3$

Associative Property of Multiplication

$(a \cdot b) \cdot c = a \cdot (b \cdot c)$ $(3 \cdot 5) \cdot 7 = 3 \cdot (5 \cdot 7)$

Commutative Property of Multiplication

$a \cdot b = b \cdot a$ $6 \cdot 3 = 3 \cdot 6$

Multiplicative Identity Property of 1

$a \cdot 1 = 1 \cdot a = a$ $8 \cdot 1 = 1 \cdot 8 = 8$

Multiplicative Inverse

For every $a \neq 0$ there exists $\frac{1}{a}$ so that $a \cdot \frac{1}{a} = \frac{1}{a} \cdot a = 1$.

For $a = 5$, $5 \cdot \frac{1}{5} = \frac{1}{5} \cdot 5 = 1$.

Distributive Property of Multiplication over Addition

$a \cdot (b + c) = (a \cdot b) + (a \cdot c)$ $2 \cdot (4 + 3) = (2 \cdot 4) + (2 \cdot 3)$

Order of Operations

Step 1 Perform operations inside parentheses.

Step 2 Simplify powers.*

Step 3 Multiply and divide from left to right.

Step 4 Add and subtract from left to right.

*Grade 5 does not include simplifying expressions with exponents.

Problem Types

Addition and Subtraction Problem Types

	Result Unknown	Change Unknown	Start Unknown
Add to	A glass contained $\frac{2}{3}$ cup of orange juice. Then $\frac{1}{4}$ cup of pineapple juice was added. How much juice is in the glass now? *Situation and solution equation:*[1] $\frac{2}{3} + \frac{1}{4} = c$	A glass contained $\frac{2}{3}$ cup of orange juice. Then some pineapple juice was added. Now the glass contains $\frac{11}{12}$ cup of juice. How much pineapple juice was added? *Situation equation:* $\frac{2}{3} + c = \frac{11}{12}$ *Solution equation:* $c = \frac{11}{12} - \frac{2}{3}$	A glass contained some orange juice. Then $\frac{1}{4}$ cup of pineapple juice was added. Now the glass contains $\frac{11}{12}$ cup of juice. How much orange juice was in the glass to start? *Situation equation* $c + \frac{1}{4} = \frac{11}{12}$ *Solution equation:* $c = \frac{11}{12} - \frac{1}{4}$
Take from	Micah had a ribbon $\frac{5}{6}$ yard long. He cut off a piece $\frac{1}{3}$ yard long. What is the length of the ribbon that is left? *Situation and solution equation:* $\frac{5}{6} - \frac{1}{3} = r$	Micah had a ribbon $\frac{5}{6}$ yard long. He cut off a piece. Now the ribbon is $\frac{1}{2}$ yard long. What is the length of the ribbon he cut off? *Situation equation:* $\frac{5}{6} - r = \frac{1}{2}$ *Solution equation:* $r = \frac{5}{6} - \frac{1}{2}$	Micah had a ribbon. He cut off a piece $\frac{1}{3}$ yard long. Now the ribbon is $\frac{1}{2}$ yard long. What was the length of the ribbon he started with? *Situation equation:* $r - \frac{1}{3} = \frac{1}{2}$ *Solution equation:* $r = \frac{1}{2} + \frac{1}{3}$

[1]A situation equation represents the structure (action) in the problem situation. A solution equation shows the operation used to find the answer.

	Total Unknown	Addend Unknown	Both Addends Unknown
Put Together/ Take Apart	A baker combines $\frac{3}{4}$ cup of white flour and $\frac{1}{2}$ cup of wheat flour. How much flour is this altogether? *Math drawing:*[2] f $\frac{3}{4}$ $\frac{1}{2}$ *Situation and solution equation:* $\frac{3}{4} + \frac{1}{2} = f$	Of the $1\frac{1}{4}$ cups of flour a baker uses, $\frac{3}{4}$ cup is white flour. The rest is wheat flour. How much wheat flour does the baker use? *Math drawing:* $1\frac{1}{4}$ $\frac{3}{4}$ f *Situation equation:* $1\frac{1}{4} = \frac{3}{4} + f$ *Solution equation:* $f = 1\frac{1}{4} - \frac{3}{4}$	A baker uses $1\frac{1}{4}$ cups of flour. Some is white flour and some is wheat flour. How much of each type of flour does the baker use? *Math drawing:* $1\frac{1}{4}$ f w *Situation equation* $1\frac{1}{4} = f + w$

[2]These math drawings are called math mountains in Grades 1–3 and break-apart drawings in Grades 4 and 5.

Problem Types continued

Addition and Subtraction Problem Types

	Difference Unknown	Greater Unknown	Smaller Unknown
Additive Comparison[1]	**Using "More"** At a zoo, the female rhino weighs $1\frac{3}{4}$ tons. The male rhino weighs $2\frac{1}{2}$ tons. How much more does the male rhino weigh than the female rhino? **Using "Less"** At a zoo, the female rhino weighs $1\frac{3}{4}$ tons. The male rhino weighs $2\frac{1}{2}$ tons. How much less does the female rhino weigh than the male rhino?	**Leading Language** At a zoo, the female rhino weighs $1\frac{3}{4}$ tons. The male rhino weighs $\frac{3}{4}$ tons more than the female rhino. How much does the male rhino weigh? **Misleading Language** At a zoo, the female rhino weighs $1\frac{3}{4}$ tons. The female rhino weighs $\frac{3}{4}$ tons less than the male rhino. How much does the male rhino weigh?	**Leading Language** At a zoo, the male rhino weighs $2\frac{1}{2}$ tons. The female rhino weighs $\frac{3}{4}$ tons less than the male rhino. How much does the female rhino weigh? **Misleading Language** At a zoo, the male rhino weighs $2\frac{1}{2}$ tons. The male rhino weighs $\frac{3}{4}$ tons more than the female rhino. How much does the female rhino weigh?

Math drawing:

Math drawing: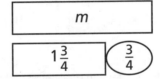

Math drawing: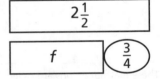

Situation equation:
$$1\frac{3}{4} + d = 2\frac{1}{2} \text{ or}$$
$$d = 2\frac{1}{2} - 1\frac{3}{4}$$
Solution equation:
$$d = 2\frac{1}{2} - 1\frac{3}{4}$$

Situation and solution equation:
$$1\frac{3}{4} + \frac{3}{4} = m$$

Situation equation
$$f + \frac{3}{4} = 2\frac{1}{2} \text{ or}$$
$$f = 2\frac{1}{2} - \frac{3}{4}$$
Solution equation:
$$f = 2\frac{1}{2} - \frac{3}{4}$$

[1]A comparison sentence can always be said in two ways. One way uses *more*, and the other uses *fewer* or *less*. Misleading language suggests the wrong operation. For example, it says the *female rhino weighs $\frac{3}{4}$ tons less than the male*, but you have to add $\frac{3}{4}$ tons to the female's weight to get the male's weight

Multiplication and Division Problem Types[1]

	Unknown Product	Group Size Unknown	Number of Groups Unknown
Equal Groups	Maddie ran around a $\frac{1}{4}$-mile track 16 times. How far did she run? *Situation and solution equation:* $n = 16 \cdot \frac{1}{4}$	Maddie ran around a track 16 times. She ran 4 miles in all. What is the distance around the track? *Situation equation:* $16 \cdot n = 4$ *Solution equation:* $n = 4 \div 16$	Maddie ran around a $\frac{1}{4}$-mile track. She ran a total distance of 4 miles. How many times did she run around the track? *Situation equation* $n \cdot \frac{1}{4} = 4$ *Solution equation:* $n = 4 \div \frac{1}{4}$

	Unknown Product	Unknown Factor	Unknown Factor
Arrays[2]	An auditorium has 58 rows with 32 seats in each row. How many seats are in the auditorium? *Math drawing:* 32 58 s *Situation and solution equation:* $s = 58 \cdot 32$	An auditorium has 58 rows with the same number of seats in each row. There are 1,856 seats in all. How many seats are in each row? *Math drawing:* s 58 1,856 *Situation equation:* $58 \cdot s = 1,856$ *Solution equation:* $s = 1,856 \div 58$	The 1,856 seats in an auditorium are arranged in rows of 32. How many rows of seats are there? *Math drawing:* 32 s 1,856 *Situation equation* $s \cdot 32 = 1,856$ *Solution equation:* $s = 1,856 \div 32$

[1]In Grade 5, students solve three types of fraction division problems: 1) They divide two whole numbers in cases where the quotient is a fraction; 2) They divide a whole number by a unit fraction; 3) They divide a unit fraction by a whole number. Fraction division with non-unit fractions is introduced in Grade 6.

[2]We use rectangle models for both array and area problems in Grades 5 and 6 because the numbers in the problems are too large to represent with arrays.

Multiplication and Division Problem Types

	Unknown Product	Unknown Factor	Unknown Factor
Area	A poster has a length of 1.2 meters and a width of 0.7 meter. What is the area of the poster? Math drawing: 1.2 0.7 A Situation and solution equation: $A = 1.2 \cdot 0.7$	A poster has an area of 0.84 square meters. The length of the poster is 1.2 meters. What is the width of the poster? Math drawing: 1.2 w 0.84 Situation equation: $1.2 \cdot w = 0.84$ Solution equation: $w = 0.84 \div 1.2$	A poster has an area of 0.84 square meters. The width of the poster is 0.7 meter. What is the length of the poster? Math drawing: l 0.7 0.84 Situation equation $l \cdot 0.7 = 0.84$ Solution equation: $l = 0.84 \div 0.7$

	Unknown Product	**Unknown Factor**	**Unknown Factor**
Multiplicative Comparison	**Whole Number Multiplier** Sam has 5 times as many goldfish as Brady has. Brady has 3 goldfish. How many goldfish does Sam have? *Math drawing:* s │ 3 ┊ 3 ┊ 3 ┊ 3 ┊ 3 b │ 3 *Situation and solution equation:* $s = 5 \cdot 3$	**Whole Number Multiplier** Sam has 5 times as many goldfish as Brady has. Sam has 15 goldfish. How many goldfish does Brady have? *Math drawing:* 15 s │ ┊ ┊ ┊ ┊ b │ *Situation equation:* $5 \cdot b = 15$ *Solution equation:* $b = 15 \div 5$	**Whole Number Multiplier** Sam has 15 goldfish. Brady has 3 goldfish. The number of goldfish Sam has is how many times the number Brady has? *Math drawing:* 15 s │ 3 ┊ 3 ┊ 3 ┊ 3 ┊ 3 b │ 3 *Situation equation* $n \cdot 3 = 15$ *Solution equation:* $n = 15 \div 3$
	Fractional Multiplier Brady has $\frac{1}{5}$ times as many goldfish as Sam has. Sam has 15 goldfish. How many goldfish does Brady have? *Math drawing:* 15 s │ ┊ ┊ ┊ ┊ b │ $\frac{1}{5}$ of 15 *Situation and solution equation:* $b = \frac{1}{5} \cdot 15$	**Fractional Multiplier** Brady has $\frac{1}{5}$ times as many goldfish as Sam has. Brady has 3 goldfish. How many goldfish does Sam have? *Math drawing:* s │ ┊ ┊ ┊ ┊ b │ 3 $\frac{1}{5}$ of s *Situation equation:* $\frac{1}{5} \cdot s = 3$ *Solution equation:* $s = 3 \div \frac{1}{5}$	**Fractional Multiplier** Sam has 15 goldfish. Brady has 3 goldfish. The number of goldfish Brady has is how many times the number Sam has? *Math drawing:* 15 s │ 3 ┊ 3 ┊ 3 ┊ 3 ┊ 3 b │ 3 *Situation equation:* $n \cdot 15 = 3$ *Solution equation:* $n = 3 \div 15$

Vocabulary Activities

MathWord Power

▶ Word Review PAIRS

Work with a partner. Choose a word from a current unit or a review word from a previous unit. Use the word to complete one of the activities listed on the right. Then ask your partner if they have any edits to your work or questions about what you described. Repeat, having your partner choose a word.

Activities

- ▶ Give the meaning in words or gestures.
- ▶ Use the word in the sentence.
- ▶ Give another word that is related to the word in some way and explain the relationship.

▶ Crossword Puzzle PAIRS OR INDIVIDUALS

Create a crossword puzzle similar to the example below. Use vocabulary words from the unit. You can add other related words, too. Challenge your partner to solve the puzzle.

Across

2. The answer to an addition problem

4. _____ and subtraction are inverse operations.

5. To put amounts together

6. When you trade 10 ones for 1 ten, you _____.

Down

1. The number to be divided in a division problem

2. The operation that you can use to find out how much more one number is than another.

3. A fraction with a numerator of 1 is a _____ fraction.

▶ Word Wall   PAIRS OR SMALL GROUPS

With your teacher's permission, start a word wall in your classroom. As you work through each lesson, put the math vocabulary words on index cards and place them on the word wall. You can work with a partner or a small group to choose a word and give the definition.

▶ Word Web   INDIVIDUALS

Make a word web for a word or words you do not understand in a unit. Fill in the web with words or phrases that are related to the vocabulary word.

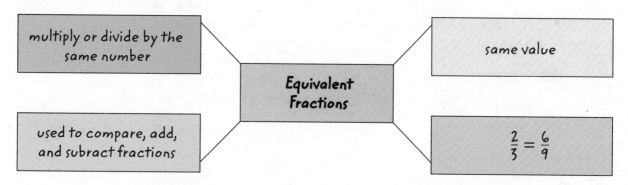

multiply or divide by the same number	Equivalent Fractions	same value
used to compare, add, and subtract fractions		$\frac{2}{3} = \frac{6}{9}$

▶ Alphabet Challenge   PAIRS OR INDIVIDUALS

Take an alphabet challenge. Choose three letters from the alphabet. Think of three vocabulary words for each letter. Then write the definition or draw an example for each word.

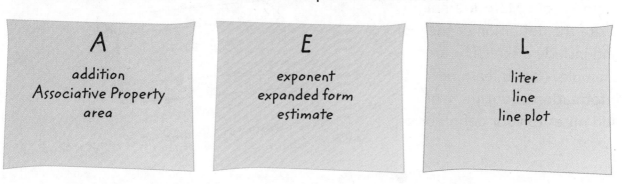

A	E	L
addition	exponent	liter
Associative Property	expanded form	line
area	estimate	line plot

Vocabulary Activities (continued)

▶ Concentration PAIRS

Write the vocabulary words and related words from a unit on index cards. Write the definitions on a different set of index cards. Mix up both sets of cards. Then place the cards facedown on a table in an array, for example, 3 by 3 or 3 by 4. Take turns turning over two cards. If one card is a word and one card is a definition that matches the word, take the pair. Continue until each word has been matched with its definition.

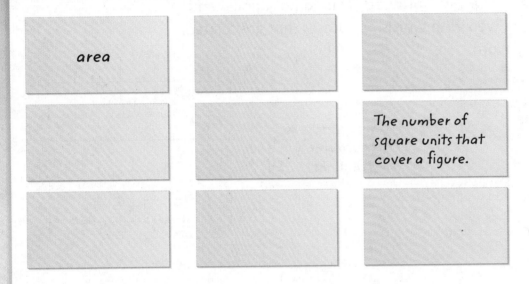

area

The number of square units that cover a figure.

▶ Math Journal INDIVIDUALS

As you learn new words, write them in your Math Journal. Write the definition of the word and include a sketch or an example. As you learn new information about the word, add notes to your definition.

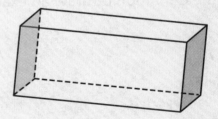

rectangular prism: a solid figure with two rectangular bases that are congruent and parallel

volume: a measure of the amount of space occupied by a solid figure

▶ What's the Word? [PAIRS]

Work together to make a poster or bulletin board display of
the words in a unit. Write definitions on a set of index cards.
Mix up the cards. Work with a partner, choosing a definition
from the index cards. Have your partner point to the word
on the poster and name the matching math vocabulary word.
Switch roles and try the activity again.

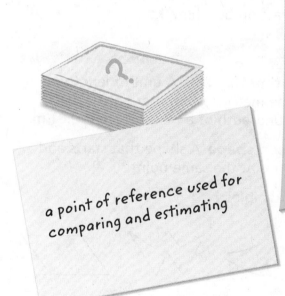

estimate

round

mixed number

equivalent fraction

common denominator

benchmark

simplify a fraction

unsimplify a fraction

unit fraction

a point of reference used for
comparing and estimating

Glossary

A

acute triangle A triangle with three acute angles.

Examples:

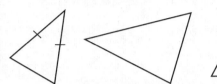

additive comparison A comparison in which one quantity is an amount greater or less than another. An additive comparison can be represented by an addition equation.

Example: Josh has 5 more goldfish than Tia.

$$j = t + 5$$

area The number of square units that cover a two-dimensional figure without gaps or overlap.

Example:

Area = 3 cm × 5 cm = 15 sq. cm

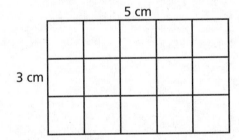

Associative Property of Addition Changing the grouping of addends does not change the sum. In symbols, $(a + b) + c = a + (b + c)$ for any numbers a, b, and c.

Example:

$$(4.7 + 2.6) + 1.4 = 4.7 + (2.6 + 1.4)$$

Associative Property of Multiplication Changing the grouping of factors does not change the product. In symbols, $(a \cdot b) \cdot c = a \cdot (b \cdot c)$ for any numbers a, b, and c.

Example:

$$(0.73 \cdot 0.2) \cdot 5 = 0.73 \cdot (0.2 \cdot 5)$$

B

base In a power, the number that is used as a repeated factor.

Example: In the power 10^3, the base is 10.

benchmark A point of reference used for comparing and estimating. The numbers 0, $\frac{1}{2}$, and 1 are common fraction benchmarks.

C

centimeter (cm) A unit of length in the metric system that equals one hundredth of a meter. 1 cm = 0.01 m.

closed shape A shape that starts and ends at the same point.

Examples:

common denominator A common multiple of two or more denominators.

Example: 18 is a common denominator of $\frac{2}{3}$ and $\frac{5}{6}$.

$$\frac{2}{3} = \frac{12}{18} \text{ and } \frac{5}{6} = \frac{15}{18}$$

Commutative Property of Addition
Changing the order of addends does not change the sum. In symbols, $a + b = b + a$ for any numbers a and b.

Example: $\frac{3}{5} + \frac{4}{9} = \frac{4}{9} + \frac{3}{5}$

Commutative Property of Multiplication Changing the order of factors does not change the product. In symbols, $a \cdot b = b \cdot a$ for any numbers a and b.

Example: $\frac{3}{7} \cdot \frac{4}{5} = \frac{4}{5} \cdot \frac{3}{7}$

comparison A statement, model, or drawing that shows the relationship between two quantities.

comparison bars Bars that represent the greater amount and the lesser amount in a comparison situation.

Example: Sarah made 2 quarts of soup. Ryan made 6 quarts. These comparison bars show that Ryan made 3 times as many quarts as Sarah.

composite number A whole number that has more than two factors.

Example: The whole number 12 is a composite number because 1, 2, 3, 4, 6, and 12 are factors of 12.

composite solid A solid figure made by combining two or more basic solid figures.

Example: The composite solid on the left below is composed of two rectangular prisms, as shown on the right.

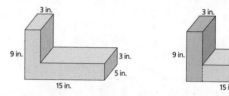

concave polygon A polygon for which you can connect two points inside the polygon with a segment that passes outside the polygon. A concave polygon has a "dent."

Examples:

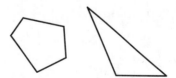

convex polygon A polygon that is not concave. All the inside angles of a convex polygon have a measure less than 180°.

Examples:

Glossary (continued)

coordinate plane A system of coordinates formed by the perpendicular intersection of horizontal and vertical number lines.

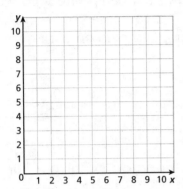

cubic unit The volume of a unit cube. A cubic unit is a unit for measuring volume.

D

decimal A number that includes a decimal point separating the whole number part of the number from the fraction part of the number.

Examples:

7.3	seven and three tenths
42.081	forty-two and eighty-one thousandths

decimeter (dm) A unit of length in the metric system that equals one tenth of a meter. 1 dm = 0.1 m.

Digit-by-Digit Method A method for solving division problems.

Example:

```
      546
  7 ) 3,822
    -3,5
    ─────
      32
     -28
    ─────
      42
     -42
```

Distributive Property of Multiplication Over Addition
Multiplying a number by a sum gives the same result as multiplying the number by each addend and then adding the products. In symbols, for all numbers a, b, and c:
$$a \times (b + c) = a \times b + a \times c$$

Example:
$$4 \times (2 + 0.75) = 4 \times 2 + 4 \times 0.75$$

dividend The number that is divided in a division problem.

Example:

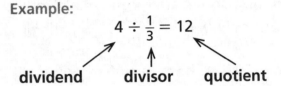

$$4 \div \frac{1}{3} = 12$$

dividend   divisor   quotient

divisor The number you divide by in a division problem.

Example:

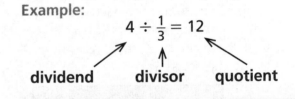

$$4 \div \frac{1}{3} = 12$$

dividend   divisor   quotient

E

edge A line segment where two faces of a three-dimensional figure meet.

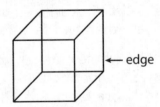

← edge

equilateral triangle A triangle with three sides of the same length.

Example:

equivalent decimals Decimals that represent the same value.

Example: 0.07 and 0.070 are equivalent decimals.

equivalent fractions Fractions that represent the same value.

Example: $\frac{1}{2}$ and $\frac{3}{6}$ are equivalent fractions.

estimate Find *about* how many or *about* how much, often by using rounding or benchmarks.

evaluate To substitute values for the variables in an expression and then simplify the resulting expression.

Example:

Evaluate $7 + 5 \cdot n$ for $n = 2$.

$7 + 5 \cdot n = 7 + 5 \cdot 2$	Substitute 2 for n.
$= 7 + 10$	Multiply.
$= 17$	Add

expanded form A way of writing a number that shows the value of each of its digits.

Example: The expanded form of 35.026 is $30 + 5 + 0.02 + 0.006$.

expanded form (powers of 10) A way of writing a number that shows the value of each of its digits using powers of 10.

Example: The expanded form of 35.026 using powers of 10 is

$(3 \times 10) + (5 \times 1) + (2 \times 0.01) + (6 + 0.001)$

Expanded Notation Method A method for solving multidigit multiplication and division problems.

Examples:

```
     43
  ×  67
  2,400
    280
    180
     21
  2,881
```

```
        6 ⎞
       40 ⎟ 546
      500 ⎠
  7 ) 3,822
     -3,500
        322
       -280
         42
        -42
```

exponent In a power, the number that tells how many times the base is used as a factor.

Example: In the power 10^3, the exponent is 3.
$$10^3 = 10 \times 10 \times 10$$

exponential form The representation of a number that uses a base and an exponent.

Example: The exponential form of 100 is 10^2.

expression A combination of one or more numbers, variables, or numbers and variables, with one or more operations.

Examples: 4

t

$6 \cdot n$

$4 \div p + 5$

$5 \times 4 + 3 \times 7$

$6 \cdot (x + 2)$

Glossary (continued)

F

face A flat surface of a three-dimensional figure.

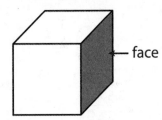

— face

factor One of two or more numbers multiplied to get a product.

Example:

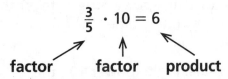

frequency table A table that shows how many times each outcome, item, or category occurs.

Example:

Outcome	Number of Students
1	6
2	3
3	5
4	4
5	2
6	5

G

greater than (>) A symbol used to show how two numbers compare. The greater number goes before the > symbol and the lesser number goes after.

Example: $\frac{2}{3} > \frac{1}{2}$ Two thirds is greater than one half.

H

hundredth A unit fraction representing one of one hundred equal parts of a whole, written as 0.01 or $\frac{1}{100}$.

I

isosceles triangle A triangle with at least two sides of the same length.

Examples:

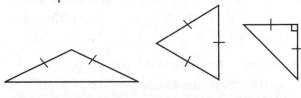

L

less than (<) A symbol used to show how two numbers compare. The lesser number goes before the < symbol and the greater number goes after.

Example: $\frac{1}{4} < \frac{1}{3}$ One fourth is less than one third.

line plot A diagram that uses a number line to show the frequency of data.

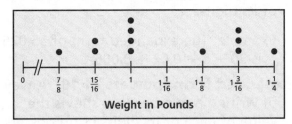

Weight in Pounds

M

meter The basic unit of length in the metric system.

mile (mi) A customary unit of length equal to 5,280 feet or 1,760 yards.

millimeter (mm) A unit of length in the metric system that equals one thousandth of a meter. 1 mm = 0.001 m.

mixed number A number with a whole number part and a fraction part.

Example: The mixed number $3\frac{2}{5}$ means $3 + \frac{2}{5}$.

multiplier The number the numerator and denominator of a fraction are multiplied by to get an equivalent fraction.

Example: A multiplier of 5 changes $\frac{2}{3}$ to $\frac{10}{15}$.

multiplicative comparison A comparison in which one quantity is a number of times the size of another. A multiplicative comparison can be represented by a multiplication equation or a division equation.

Example: Tomás picked 3 times as many apples as Catie.

$$t = 3 \cdot c$$
$$t \div 3 = c \text{ or } \frac{1}{3} \cdot t = c$$

New Groups Below Method A method used to solve multidigit multiplication problems.

Example:

$$\begin{array}{r} 67 \\ \times\ 43 \\ \hline \scriptstyle 1\,2 \\ 81 \\ \scriptstyle 2\ 2 \\ 480 \\ \scriptstyle 1 \\ \hline 2{,}881 \end{array}$$

numerical pattern A sequence of numbers that share a relationship.

Example: In this numerical pattern, each term is 3 more than the term before.

2, 5, 8, 11, 14, . . .

obtuse triangle A triangle with an obtuse angle.

Examples:

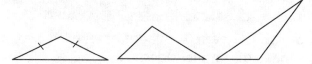

one-dimensional figure A figure with only one dimension, usually length.

Examples:

open shape A shape that does not start and end at the same point.

Examples:

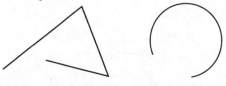

Order of Operations A rule that states the order in which the operations in an expression should be done:

Step 1 Perform operations inside parentheses.

Step 2 Multiply and divide from left to right.

Step 3 Add and subtract from left to right.

ordered pair A pair of numbers that shows the position of a point on a coordinate plane.

Example: The ordered pair (3, 4) represents a point 3 units to the right of the y-axis and 4 units above the x-axis.

Glossary (continued)

origin The point (0, 0) on the coordinate plane.

overestimate An estimate that is too big.

P

parallelogram A quadrilateral with two pairs of parallel sides.

Examples:

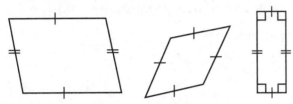

partial products In a multidigit multiplication problem, the products obtained by multiplying each place value of one factor by each place value of the other.

Example: In the problem below, the partial products are in red.

$$25 \cdot 53 = 20 \cdot 50 + 20 \cdot 3 + 5 \cdot 50 + 5 \cdot 3$$

perimeter The distance around a figure.

Example:

Perimeter = 2 · 3 cm + 2 · 5 cm = 16 cm

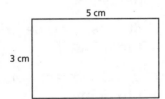

Place Value Rows Method A method used to solve multidigit multiplication problems.

Example:

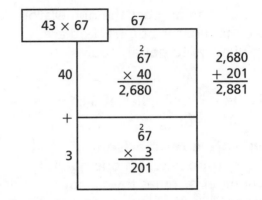

Place Value Sections Method A method used to solve multidigit multiplication and division problems.

Examples:

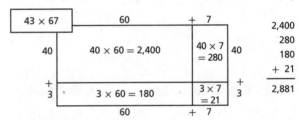

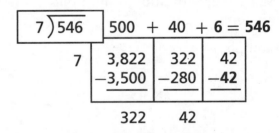

polygon A closed two-dimensional shape made from line segments that do not cross each other.

Examples:

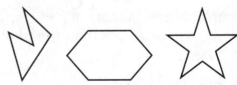

power of 10 A power with a base of 10. A number in the form 10^n.

Examples: 10^1, 10^2, 10^3

prime number A whole number that has exactly two factors—the number itself and 1.

Examples: The whole number 13 is a prime number because the only factors of 13 are 1 and 13. The whole number 1 is neither prime nor composite.

product The result of a multiplication.

Example:

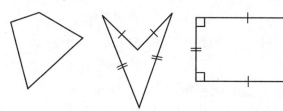

$$\frac{3}{5} \cdot 10 = 6$$

factor   factor   product

Q

quadrilateral A closed two-dimensional shape with four straight sides.

Examples:

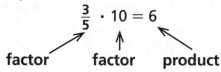

quotient The answer to a division problem.

Example:

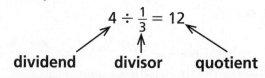

$$4 \div \frac{1}{3} = 12$$

dividend   divisor   quotient

R

rectangle A parallelogram with four right angles.

Examples:

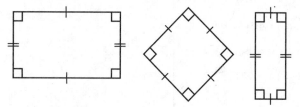

rectangular prism A solid figure with two rectangular bases that are congruent and parallel.

Example:

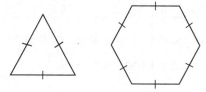

regular polygon A polygon in which all sides and all angles are congruent.

Examples:

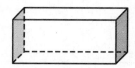

Glossary (continued)

remainder The number left over when a divisor does not divide evenly into a dividend.

Example:

$$
\begin{array}{r}
13 \\
7\overline{)94} \\
-7 \\
\hline
24 \\
21 \\
\hline
3 \leftarrow \text{remainder}
\end{array}
$$

rhombus A parallelogram with four congruent sides.

Examples:

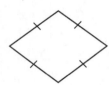

right triangle A triangle with a right angle.

Examples:

round To change a number to a nearby number.

Examples:

54.72 rounded to the nearest ten is 50.

54.72 rounded to the nearest one is 55.

54.72 rounded to the nearest tenth is 54.7.

$3\frac{7}{9}$ rounded to the nearest whole number is 4.

scalene triangle A triangle with no sides of the same length.

Examples:

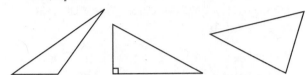

shift To change position. When we multiply a decimal or whole number by 10, 100, or 1,000, the digits shift to the left. When we divide by 10, 100, or 1,000, the digits shift to the right. When we multiply by 0.1, 0.01, or 0.001, the digits shift to the right. When we divide by 0.1, 0.01, or 0.001, the digits shift to the left.

Examples:

$72.4 \times 100 = 7{,}240$ Digits shift left 2 places.

$5.04 \div 10 = 0.504$ Digits shift right 1 place.

$729 \times 0.01 = 7.29$ Digits shift right 2 places.

$0.26 \div 0.001 = 260$ Digits shift left 3 places.

Short Cut Method A method used to solve multidigit multiplication problems.

Example:

$$
\begin{array}{r}
\overset{1}{\underset{}{\overset{2}{43}}} \\
\times\ 67 \\
\hline
301 \\
2{,}580 \\
\hline
2{,}881
\end{array}
$$

simplify a fraction Make an equivalent fraction by dividing the numerator and denominator of a fraction by the same number. Simplifying makes fewer but larger parts.

Example: Simplify $\frac{12}{16}$ by dividing the numerator and denominator by 4.

$$\frac{12 \div 4}{16 \div 4} = \frac{3}{4}$$

simplify an expression Use the Order of Operations to find the value of the expression.

Example: Simplify $6 \cdot (2 + 5) \div 3$.

$$
\begin{aligned}
6 \cdot (2 + 5) \div 3 \quad &= 6 \cdot 7 \div 3 \\
&= 42 \div 3 \\
&= 14
\end{aligned}
$$

situation equation An equation that shows the action or the relationship in a word problem.

Example:

Liam has some change in his pocket. He spends 25¢. Now he has 36¢ in his pocket. How much change did he have to start?

situation equation: $x - 25 = 36$

solution equation An equation that shows the operation to perform in order to solve a word problem.

Example:

Liam has some change in his pocket. He spends 25¢. Now he has 36¢ in his pocket. How much change did he have to start?

solution equation: $x = 36 + 25$

square A rectangle with four congruent sides. (Or, a rhombus with four right angles.)

Examples:

standard form The form of a number using digits, in which the place of each digit indicates its value.

Example: 407.65

T

tenth A unit fraction representing one of ten equal parts of a whole, written as 0.1 or $\frac{1}{10}$.

term Each number in a numerical pattern.

Example: In the pattern below, 3 is the first term, and 9 is the fourth term.

3, 5, 7, 9, 11, . . .

thousandth A unit fraction representing one of one thousand equal parts of a whole, written as 0.001 or $\frac{1}{1,000}$.

three-dimensional figure A figure with three dimensions, usually length, width, and height.

Examples:

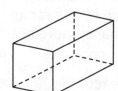

Glossary (continued)

ton (T) A customary unit of weight that equals 2,000 pounds.

trapezoid A quadrilateral with exactly one pair of parallel sides.

Examples:

two-dimensional figure A figure with two dimensions, usually length and width.

Examples:

U

underestimate An estimate that is too small.

unit cube A cube with sides lengths of 1 unit.

1 unit
1 unit
1 unit

unit fraction A fraction with a numerator of 1. A unit fraction is one equal part of a whole.

Examples: $\frac{1}{3}$ and $\frac{1}{12}$

unsimplify Make an equivalent fraction by multiplying the numerator and denominator of a fraction by the same number. Unsimplifying makes more but smaller parts.

Example: Unsimplify $\frac{3}{4}$ by multiplying the numerator and denominator by 2.

$$\frac{3 \times 2}{4 \times 2} = \frac{6}{8}$$

V

variable A letter or other symbol used to stand for an unknown number in an algebraic expression.

volume A measure of the amount of space occupied by a solid figure. Volume is measured in cubic units.

W

word form The form of a number that uses words instead of digits.

Example: twelve and thirty-two hundredths

X

x-axis The horizontal axis of the coordinate plane.

x-coordinate The first number in an ordered pair, which represents a point's horizontal distance from the *y*-axis.

Example: The *x*-coordinate of the point represented by the ordered pair (3, 4) is 3.

Y

y-axis The vertical axis of the coordinate plane.

y-coordinate The second number in an ordered pair, which represents a point's vertical distance from the *x*-axis.

Example: The *y*-coordinate of the point represented by the ordered pair (3, 4) is 4.

California Common Core Standards for Mathematical Content

5.OA Operations and Algebraic Thinking

Write and interpret numerical expressions.

5.OA.1	Use parentheses, brackets, or braces in numerical expressions, and evaluate them with these symbols.	Unit 6 Lesson 8; Unit 7 Lessons 1, 2, 3, 4, 7
5.OA.2	Write simple expressions that record calculations with numbers, and interpret numerical expressions without evaluating them.	Unit 7 Lessons 1, 3, 4
5.OA.2.1	Express a whole number in the range 2–50 as a product of its prime factors.	Unit 7 Lesson 4

Analyze patterns and relationships.

5.OA.3	Generate two numerical patterns using two given rules. Identify apparent relationships between corresponding terms. Form ordered pairs consisting of corresponding terms from the two patterns, and graph the ordered pairs on a coordinate plane.	Unit 7 Lessons 4, 6

5.NBT Number and Operations in Base Ten

Understand the place value system.

5.NBT.1	Recognize that in a multi-digit number, a digit in one place represents 10 times as much as it represents in the place to its right and $\frac{1}{10}$ of what it represents in the place to its left.	Unit 2 Lessons 2, 3; Unit 4 Lessons 1, 3, 7, 9
5.NBT.2	Explain patterns in the number of zeros of the product when multiplying a number by powers of 10, and explain patterns in the placement of the decimal point when a decimal is multiplied or divided by a power of 10. Use whole-number exponents to denote powers of 10.	Unit 4 Lessons 1, 2, 6, 7, 9; Unit 5 Lessons 6, 7, 8
5.NBT.3	Read, write, and compare decimals to thousandths.	Unit 2 Lessons 1, 2, 3; Unit 4 Lesson 12
5.NBT.3a	Read and write decimals to thousandths using base-ten numerals, number names, and expanded form, e.g., $347.392 = 3 \times 100 + 4 \times 10 + 7 \times 1 + 3 \times (\frac{1}{10}) + 9 \times (\frac{1}{100}) + 2 \times (\frac{1}{1000})$.	Unit 2 Lessons 1, 2, 3
5.NBT.3b	Compare two decimals to thousandths based on meanings of the digits in each place, using >, =, and < symbols to record the results of comparisons.	Unit 2 Lessons 3, 9; Unit 4 Lesson 12; Unit 5 Lesson 10
5.NBT.4	Use place value understanding to round decimals to any place.	Unit 2 Lessons 8, 9; Unit 4 Lesson 10; Unit 6 Lesson 4

Perform operations with multi-digit whole numbers and with decimals to hundredths.

5.NBT.5	Fluently multiply multi-digit whole numbers using the standard algorithm.	Unit 4 Lessons 3, 4, 5, 8, 11, 12; Unit 5 Lesson 10; Unit 6 Lessons 2, 5, 6, 7, 8, 9
5.NBT.6	Find whole-number quotients of whole numbers with up to four-digit dividends and two-digit divisors, using strategies based on place value, the properties of operations, and/or the relationship between multiplication and division. Illustrate and explain the calculation by using equations, rectangular arrays, and/or area models.	Unit 5 Lessons 1, 2, 3, 4, 5, 9, 10; Unit 6 Lessons 2, 4, 6, 7, 9, 10
5.NBT.7	Add, subtract, multiply, and divide decimals to hundredths, using concrete models or drawings and strategies based on place value, properties of operations, and/or the relationship between addition and subtraction; relate the strategy to a written method and explain the reasoning used.	Unit 2 Lessons 4, 5, 6, 7, 10; Unit 4 Lessons 1, 6, 7, 8, 9, 10, 11, 12; Unit 5 Lessons 6, 7, 8, 9, 10, 11; Unit 6 Lessons 1, 2, 4, 6, 7, 8, 9, 11

5.NF Number and Operations–Fractions

Use equivalent fractions as a strategy to add and subtract fractions.

5.NF.1	Add and subtract fractions with unlike denominators (including mixed numbers) by replacing given fractions with equivalent fractions in such a way as to produce an equivalent sum or difference of fractions with like denominators.	Unit 1 Lessons 2, 3, 4, 5, 7, 8, 9, 10, 11, 12, 13; Unit 3 Lessons 7, 8, 13; Unit 6 Lesson 4
5.NF.2	Solve word problems involving addition and subtraction of fractions referring to the same whole, including cases of unlike denominators, e.g., by using visual fraction models or equations to represent the problem. Use benchmark fractions and number sense of fractions to estimate mentally and assess the reasonableness of answers.	Unit 1 Lessons 1, 6, 7, 8, 9, 10, 11, 12, 13; Unit 3 Lessons 7, 8, 13; Unit 6 Lessons 1, 4, 7, 8, 9, 10

Apply and extend previous understandings of multiplication and division to multiply and divide fractions.

5.NF.3	Interpret a fraction as division of the numerator by the denominator ($\frac{a}{b} = a \div b$). Solve word problems involving division of whole numbers leading to answers in the form of fractions or mixed numbers, e.g., by using visual fraction models or equations to represent the problem.	Unit 3 Lessons 10, 11, 13, 14; Unit 6 Lesson 11
5.NF.4	Apply and extend previous understandings of multiplication to multiply a fraction or whole number by a fraction.	Unit 3 Lessons 1, 2, 3, 4, 5, 6, 7, 8, 9, 10, 12, 13; Unit 6 Lesson 2
5.NF.4a	Interpret the product $(\frac{a}{b}) \times q$ as a parts of a partition of q into b equal parts; equivalently, as the result of a sequence of operations $a \times q \div b$.	Unit 3 Lessons 1, 2, 3, 4, 5, 7, 10; Unit 6 Lesson 3

5.NF.4b	Find the area of a rectangle with fractional side lengths by tiling it with unit squares of the appropriate unit fraction side lengths, and show that the area is the same as would be found by multiplying the side lengths. Multiply fractional side lengths to find areas of rectangles, and represent fraction products as rectangular areas.	Unit 3 Lessons 4, 6; Unit 6 Lesson 2; Unit 8 Lesson 8
5.NF.5	Interpret multiplication as scaling (resizing), by:	Unit 3 Lessons 1, 6, 7, 8, 9, 12, 13; Unit 4 Lesson 12; Unit 5 Lesson 10; Unit 6 Lesson 6
5.NF.5a	Comparing the size of a product to the size of one factor on the basis of the size of the other factor, without performing the indicated multiplication.	Unit 3 Lessons 6, 7, 8, 9, 12, 13, 14; Unit 4 Lesson 12; Unit 5 Lesson 10; Unit 6 Lesson 6
5.NF.5b	Explaining why multiplying a given number by a fraction greater than 1 results in a product greater than the given number (recognizing multiplication by whole numbers greater than 1 as a familiar case); explaining why multiplying a given number by a fraction less than 1 results in a product smaller than the given number; and relating the principle of fraction equivalence $\frac{a}{b} = \frac{(n \times a)}{(n \times b)}$ to the effect of multiplying $\frac{a}{b}$ by 1.	Unit 3 Lessons 1, 6, 7, 9, 12; Unit 4 Lesson 12; Unit 6 Lesson 6
5.NF.6	Solve real world problems involving multiplication of fractions and mixed numbers, e.g., by using visual fraction models or equations to represent the problem.	Unit 3 Lessons 1, 2, 3, 4, 5, 6, 7, 8, 9, 12, 13, 14; Unit 6 Lessons 2, 6, 8, 9, 10
5.NF.7	Apply and extend previous understandings of division to divide unit fractions by whole numbers and whole numbers by unit fractions.	Unit 3 Lessons 10, 11, 12, 13; Unit 6 Lesson 2
5.NF.7a	Interpret division of a unit fraction by a non-zero whole number, and compute such quotients.	Unit 3 Lessons 10, 11, 12, 13; Unit 6 Lesson 3
5.NF.7b	Interpret division of a whole number by a unit fraction, and compute such quotients.	Unit 3 Lessons 10, 11, 12, 13; Unit 6 Lesson 3
5.NF.7c	Solve real world problems involving division of unit fractions by non-zero whole numbers and division of whole numbers by unit fractions, e.g., by using visual fraction models and equations to represent the problem.	Unit 3 Lessons 10, 11, 12, 13, 14; Unit 6 Lessons 2, 6, 8, 10

5.MD Measurement and Data

Convert like measurement units within a given measurement system.

5.MD.1	Convert among different-sized standard measurement units within a given measurement system (e.g., convert 5 cm to 0.05 m), and use these conversions in solving multi-step, real world problems.	Unit 2 Lesson 4; Unit 8 Lessons 1, 2, 3, 4, 5, 6

Represent and interpret data.

5.MD.2	Make a line plot to display a data set of in fractions of a unit $(\frac{1}{2}, \frac{1}{4}, \frac{1}{8})$. Use operations on fractions for this grade to solve problems involving information presented in line plots.	Unit 1 Lesson 10; Unit 3 Lesson 13; Unit 8 Lesson 7

Geometric measurement: understand concepts of volume and relate volume to multiplication and to addition.

5.MD.3	Recognize volume as an attribute of solid figures and understand concepts of volume measurement.	Unit 8 Lessons 10, 17
5.MD.3a	A cube with side length 1 unit, called a "unit cube," is said to have "one cubic unit" of volume, and can be used to measure volume.	Unit 8 Lessons 9, 10
5.MD.3b	A solid figure which can be packed without gaps or overlaps using n unit cubes is said to have a volume of n cubic units.	Unit 8 Lessons 9, 10
5.MD.4	Measure volumes by counting unit cubes, using cubic cm, cubic in., cubic ft, and improvised units.	Unit 8 Lessons 9, 11
5.MD.5	Relate volume to the operations of multiplication and addition and solve real world and mathematical problems involving volume.	Unit 8 Lessons 13, 17
5.MD.5a	Find the volume of a right rectangular prism with whole-number side lengths by packing it with unit cubes, and show that the volume is the same as would be found by multiplying the edge lengths, equivalently by multiplying the height by the area of the base. Represent threefold whole-number products as volumes, e.g., to represent the associative property of multiplication.	Unit 8 Lessons 9, 11
5.MD.5b	Apply the formulas $V = l \times w \times h$ and $V = b \times h$ for rectangular prisms to find volumes of right rectangular prisms with whole number edge lengths in the context of solving real world and mathematical problems.	Unit 8 Lessons 11, 12, 13, 17
5.MD.5c	Recognize volume as additive. Find volumes of solid figures composed of two non-overlapping right rectangular prisms by adding the volumes of the non-overlapping parts, applying this technique to solve real world problems.	Unit 8 Lesson 13

Graph points on the coordinate plane to solve real-world and mathematical problems.

5.G.1	Use a pair of perpendicular number lines, called axes, to define a coordinate system, with the intersection of the lines (the origin) arranged to coincide with the 0 on each line and a given point in the plane located by using an ordered pair of numbers, called its coordinates.Understand that the first number indicates how far to travel from the origin in the direction of one axis, and the second number indicates how far to travel in the direction of the second axis, with the convention that the names of the two axes and the coordinates correspond (e.g., x-axis and x-coordinate, y-axis and y-coordinate).	Unit 7 Lessons 5, 6, 7
5.G.2	Represent real world and mathematical problems by graphing points in the first quadrant of the coordinate plane, and interpret coordinate values of points in the context of the situation.	Unit 7 Lessons 6, 7

Classify two-dimensional figures into categories based on their properties.

5.G.3	Understand that attributes belonging to a category of two-dimensional figures also belong to all subcategories of that category.	Unit 8 Lessons 14, 15, 16
5.G.4	Classify two-dimensional figures in a hierarchy based on properties.	Unit 8 Lessons 14, 15, 16

California Common Core Standards for Mathematical Practice

MP.1 Make sense of problems and persevere in solving them.

Mathematically proficient students start by explaining to themselves the meaning of a problem and looking for entry points to its solution. They analyze givens, constraints, relationships, and goals. They make conjectures about the form and meaning of the solution and plan a solution pathway rather than simply jumping into a solution attempt. They consider analogous problems, and try special cases and simpler forms of the original problem in order to gain insight into its solution. They monitor and evaluate their progress and change course if necessary. Older students might, depending on the context of the problem, transform algebraic expressions or change the viewing window on their graphing calculator to get the information they need. Mathematically proficient students can explain correspondences between equations, verbal descriptions, tables, and graphs or draw diagrams of important features and relationships, graph data, and search for regularity or trends. Younger students might rely on using concrete objects or pictures to help conceptualize and solve a problem. Mathematically proficient students check their answers to problems using a different method, and they continually ask themselves, "Does this make sense?" They can understand the approaches of others to solving complex problems and identify correspondences between different approaches.

Unit 1 Lessons 1, 7, 8, 9, 12, 13; Unit 2 Lessons 4, 6, 8, 9, 10; Unit 3 Lessons 1, 2, 3, 4, 5, 6, 7, 8, 9, 10, 11, 12, 13, 14; Unit 4 Lessons 1, 3, 6, 7, 8, 11, 12; Unit 5 Lessons 1, 2, 4, 6, 7, 8, 9, 10, 11; Unit 6 Lessons 1, 2, 4, 5, 6, 7, 8, 9, 10, 11; Unit 7 Lessons 3, 4, 6, 7; Unit 8 Lessons 1, 2, 3, 4, 5, 6, 11, 13, 15, 17

MP.2 Reason abstractly and quantitatively.

Mathematically proficient students make sense of quantities and their relationships in problem situations. They bring two complementary abilities to bear on problems involving quantitative relationships: the ability to *decontextualize*—to abstract a given situation and represent it symbolically and manipulate the representing symbols as if they have a life of their own, without necessarily attending to their referents—and the ability to *contextualize*, to pause as needed during the manipulation process in order to probe into the referents for the symbols involved. Quantitative reasoning entails habits of creating a coherent representation of the problem at hand; considering the units involved; attending to the meaning of quantities, not just how to compute them; and knowing and flexibly using different properties of operations and objects.

Unit 1 Lessons 1, 2, 3, 4, 5, 7, 8, 13; Unit 2 Lessons 1, 2, 3, 4, 5, 8, 10; Unit 3 Lessons 3, 4, 5, 6, 7, 8, 10, 11, 12, 14; Unit 4 Lessons 1, 3, 7, 9, 10, 11, 12; Unit 5 Lessons 1, 3, 7, 8, 9, 10, 11; Unit 6 Lessons 1, 2, 3, 5, 6, 11; Unit 7 Lessons 1, 4, 5, 6, 7; Unit 8 Lessons 1, 4, 5, 6, 10, 17

MP.3 Construct viable arguments and critique the reasoning of others.

Mathematically proficient students understand and use stated assumptions, definitions, and previously established results in constructing arguments. They make conjectures and build a logical progression of statements to explore the truth of their conjectures. They are able to analyze situations by breaking them into cases, and can recognize and use counterexamples. They justify their conclusions, communicate them to others, and respond to the arguments of others. They reason inductively about data, making plausible arguments that take into account the context from which the data arose. Mathematically proficient students are also able to compare the effectiveness of two plausible arguments, distinguish correct logic or reasoning from that which is flawed, and—if there is a flaw in an argument—explain what it is. Elementary students can construct arguments using concrete referents such as objects, drawings, diagrams, and actions. Such arguments can make sense and be correct, even though they are not generalized or made formal until later grades. Later, students learn to determine domains to which an argument applies. Students at all grades can listen or read the arguments of others, decide whether they make sense, and ask useful questions to clarify or improve the arguments.

Unit 1 Lessons 1, 2, 3, 4, 5, 6, 7, 8, 9, 10, 11, 12, 13; Unit 2 Lessons 1, 2, 3, 4, 5, 6, 7, 8, 9, 10; Unit 3 Lessons 1, 2, 3, 4, 5, 6, 7, 8, 9, 10, 11, 12, 13, 14; Unit 4 Lessons 1, 2, 3, 4, 6, 7, 8, 9, 10, 11, 12; Unit 5 Lessons 1, 2, 3, 4, 5, 6, 7, 8, 9, 10, 11; Unit 6 Lessons 1, 2, 3, 4, 5, 6, 7, 8, 9, 10, 11; Unit 7 Lessons 1, 2, 3, 4, 5, 6, 7; Unit 8 Lessons 1, 2, 3, 4, 5, 6, 7, 8, 9, 10, 11, 12, 13, 14, 15, 16, 17

MP.4 Model with mathematics.

Mathematically proficient students can apply the mathematics they know to solve problems arising in everyday life, society, and the workplace. In early grades, this might be as simple as writing an addition equation to describe a situation. In middle grades, a student might apply proportional reasoning to plan a school event or analyze a problem in the community. By high school, a student might use geometry to solve a design problem or use a function to describe how one quantity of interest depends on another. Mathematically proficient students who can apply what they know are comfortable making assumptions and approximations to simplify a complicated situation, realizing that these may need revision later. They are able to identify important quantities in a practical situation and map their relationships using such tools as diagrams, two-way tables, graphs, flowcharts and formulas. They can analyze those relationships mathematically to draw conclusions. They routinely interpret their mathematical results in the context of the situation and reflect on whether the results make sense, possibly improving the model if it has not served its purpose.

Unit 1 Lessons 1, 3, 5, 6, 7, 8, 9, 12, 13; Unit 2 Lessons 4, 9, 10; Unit 3 Lessons 1, 2, 4, 10, 11, 14; Unit 4 Lessons 1, 2, 3, 6, 12; Unit 5 Lessons 1, 2, 6, 11; Unit 6 Lessons 1, 2, 3, 4, 5, 6, 7, 8, 10, 11; Unit 7 Lessons 3, 6, 7; Unit 8 Lessons 7, 9, 10, 15, 17

MP.5 Use appropriate tools strategically.

Mathematically proficient students consider the available tools when solving a mathematical problem. These tools might include pencil and paper, concrete models, a ruler, a protractor, a calculator, a spreadsheet, a computer algebra system, a statistical package, or dynamic geometry software. Proficient students are sufficiently familiar with tools appropriate for their grade or course to make sound decisions about when each of these tools might be helpful, recognizing both the insight to be gained and their limitations. For example, mathematically proficient high school students analyze graphs of functions and solutions generated using a graphing calculator. They detect possible errors by strategically using estimation and other mathematical knowledge. When making mathematical models, they know that technology can enable them to visualize the results of varying assumptions, explore consequences, and compare predictions with data. Mathematically proficient students at various grade levels are able to identify relevant external mathematical resources, such as digital content located on a website, and use them to pose or solve problems. They are able to use technological tools to explore and deepen their understanding of concepts.

Unit 1 Lessons 1, 2, 3, 4, 5, 13; Unit 2 Lessons 2, 3, 4, 6, 8, 10; Unit 3 Lessons 3, 4, 10, 11, 14; Unit 4 Lessons 1, 12; Unit 5 Lessons 6, 11; Unit 6 Lessons 3, 11; Unit 7 Lessons 5, 6, 7; Unit 8 Lessons 7, 9, 11, 14, 15, 16, 17

MP.6 Attend to precision.

Mathematically proficient students try to communicate precisely to others. They try to use clear definitions in discussion with others and in their own reasoning. They state the meaning of the symbols they choose, including using the equal sign consistently and appropriately. They are careful about specifying units of measure, and labeling axes to clarify the correspondence with quantities in a problem. They calculate accurately and efficiently, express numerical answers with a degree of precision appropriate for the problem context. In the elementary grades, students give carefully formulated explanations to each other. By the time they reach high school they have learned to examine claims and make explicit use of definitions.

Unit 1 Lessons 1, 2, 3, 4, 5, 6, 7, 8, 9, 10, 11, 12, 13; Unit 2 Lessons 1, 2, 3, 4, 5, 6, 7, 8, 9, 10; Unit 3 Lessons 1, 2, 3, 4, 5, 6, 7, 8, 9, 10, 11, 12, 13, 14; Unit 4 Lessons 1, 2, 3, 4, 5, 6, 7, 8, 9, 10, 11, 12; Unit 5 Lessons 1, 2, 3, 4, 5, 6, 7, 8, 9, 10, 11; Unit 6 Lessons 1, 2, 3, 4, 5, 6, 7, 8, 9, 10, 11; Unit 7 Lessons 1, 2, 3, 4, 5, 6, 7; Unit 8 Lessons 1, 2, 3, 4, 5, 6, 7, 8, 9, 10, 11, 12, 13, 14, 15, 16, 17

MP.7 Look for and make use of structure.

Mathematically proficient students look closely to discern a pattern or structure. Young students, for example, might notice that three and seven more is the same amount as seven and three more, or they may sort a collection of shapes according to how many sides the shapes have. Later, students will see 7×8 equals the well remembered $7 \times 5 + 7 \times 3$, in preparation for learning about the distributive property. In the expression $x^2 + 9x + 14$, older students can see the 14 as 2×7 and the 9 as $2 + 7$. They recognize the significance of an existing line in a geometric figure and can use the strategy of drawing an auxiliary line for solving problems. They also can step back for an overview and shift perspective. They can see complicated things, such as some algebraic expressions, as single objects or as being composed of several objects. For example, they can see $5 - 3(x - y)^2$ as 5 minus a positive number times a square and use that to realize that its value cannot be more than 5 for any real numbers x and y.

Unit 1 Lessons 1, 2, 3, 4, 9, 10, 12, 13; Unit 2 Lessons 1, 3, 4, 7, 10; Unit 3 Lessons 1, 2, 4, 6, 7, 10, 14; Unit 4 Lessons 2, 4, 6, 7, 8, 9, 12; Unit 5 Lessons 1, 6, 8, 9, 11; Unit 6 Lessons 2, 4, 6, 7, 11; Unit 7 Lessons 2, 4, 5, 7; Unit 8 Lessons 1, 2, 5, 6, 9, 14, 15, 16, 17

MP.8 Look for and express regularity in repeated reasoning.

Mathematically proficient students notice if calculations are repeated, and look both for general methods and for shortcuts. Upper elementary students might notice when dividing 25 by 11 that they are repeating the same calculations over and over again, and conclude they have a repeating decimal. By paying attention to the calculation of slope as they repeatedly check whether points are on the line through (1, 2) with slope 3, middle school students might abstract the equation $(y - 2)/(x - 1) = 3$. Noticing the regularity in the way terms cancel when expanding $(x - 1)(x + 1)$, $(x - 1)(x^2 + x + 1)$, and $(x - 1)(x^3 + x^2 + x + 1)$ might lead them to the general formula for the sum of a geometric series. As they work to solve a problem, mathematically proficient students maintain oversight of the process, while attending to the details. They continually evaluate the reasonableness of their intermediate results.

Unit 1 Lessons 3, 4, 7, 8, 9, 10, 13; Unit 2 Lessons 1, 2, 3, 7, 8, 10; Unit 3 Lessons 2, 3, 4, 6, 7, 9, 10, 12, 13, 14; Unit 4 Lessons 1, 2, 6, 7, 8, 9, 11, 12; Unit 5 Lessons 1, 3, 6, 7, 10, 11; Unit 6 Lessons 4, 6, 11; Unit 7 Lessons 3, 4, 5, 7; Unit 8 Lessons 2, 3, 7, 8, 13, 17

Index

A

Acute angle, 250

Addend, 51

Addition

comparison bars in, 219

of decimals, 47–48

estimating sums, 54

of fractions, 17–18, 25–26, 87, 101–102

methods, 21

of mixed numbers, 15, 22, 24

properties of, 51–52

  Associative, 51–52

  Commutative, 52

regrouping and reordering of, 51

situations, 27, 207–208

  convert to solution equations, 27,
    207–208

Algebra

coordinate plane

  distance and the, 251–252

  ordered pairs, 249–250

    graphing, 253–254

  patterns on, 253–254

  plot points, 250–251, 253–254

  x-axis and y-axis, 249–256

equations

  fractions and, 86, 209

  solving addition and subtraction
    equations, 207

  solving multiplication and division
    equations, 209

  using a variable to represent an
    unknown, 247

  writing, 91, 96, 221, 245, 280

expressions

  defined, 239

  evaluating, 243–244

    by substitution, 243–244

  using order of operations, 221–222,
    240, 241

  inverse relationships, 91–94

  using parentheses, 42, 51, 221, 242

  using properties, 143–144, 288, 289

  writing, 239–240, 244, 287

inverse operations, 91–94

patterns. *See* Patterns

properties

  Associative

    of addition, 51–52

    of multiplication, 85, 143–144,
      288, 289

  Commutative

    of addition, 52

    of multiplication, 84, 98, 143–144,
      288, 289

  Distributive, 51–52, 85, 123

  term, 245–246, 253

  using order of operations, 221–222,
    227, 240

  using parentheses, 42, 51, 221–222, 242

  variables, 239, 243, 247

  Venn diagrams, 298

Angle, 250

acute, 250

Area, 291–292

compare array and, 123

formulas for, 281–284

of rectangles, 95, 209, 281–284

Area model, 76, 81, 84, 128

Array

defined, 123

real world situations, 128, 167

Assessment

Assessment Resources, 31–36, 59–64,
  105–110, 155–160, 199–204, 231–236,
  257–262, 303–308

Formative Assessment, In every
TE Lesson
Check Understanding, In every
TE Lesson
Reteaching Resources, 31–36, 59–64,
105–110, 155–160, 199–204, 231–236,
257–262, 303–308
Summative Assessment
Unit Assessment Overview, 31–36,
59–64, 105–110, 155–160, 199–204,
231–236, 257–262, 303–308
Unit Review and Test, 31–36, 59–64,
105–110, 155–160, 199–204,
231–236, 257–262, 303–308

Associative Property of Addition,
51–52

Associative Property of Multiplication,
85, 143–144, 288, 289

Attribute Cards, 300C–300D

B

Bar graph
making, 56, 230
Benchmarks
for fractions, 11, 214
Break-apart
drawings, 207–208

C

California Common Core Standards.
See **California Common Core Standard**
correlations on the first page of every
lesson

California Common Core
Mathematical Content Standards.
S25–S29

California Common Core
Mathematical Practice Standards.
S30–S33

Capacity, 269–270, 275–276. *See also*
Liquid Volume

Centimeter, 45, 46

Common denominator, 10, 12, 18,
22, 23

Common factor, 18

Common multiple, 18

Commutative Property
of Addition, 52
of Multiplication, 84, 98, 143–144,
288, 289
with fractions, 83, 84

Compare
customary and metric measures, 275
decimals, 44, 56
fractions and mixed numbers, 3,
9–12, 87

Comparison situations, 95
in addition and subtraction, 19–20, 215,
219–220
leading language in, 215–216
misleading language in, 215–216
in multiplication, 68–70, 82, 216–220

Content Overview, 1–2, 37–38, 65–66,
111–112, 161–162, 205–206, 237–238,
263–264

Coordinate plane, 249–252
axis, 251, 253–255
distance and the, 251–252
locate points, 249, 252
ordered pairs, 249–250
graphing, 253–254
patterns on, 253–254

plot points, 250–251, 253–254

real world, 254

x-axis and y-axis, 249–256

Coordinate Plane Poster. *See* **Manipulatives**

Counterexample, 295, 297

Cup, 275

Customary measurement. *See* **Measurement, customary**

D

Data

graph, 55–56

line plot, 24, 102, 279–280

Decimals

add, 47–48

compare, 44, 56

  connect to fractions, 185

  operations, 194

  order and, 56

convert to fractions, 185

divide, 177–190, 193–196

equivalent, 43

estimate, 54

expanded form, 42

fractions and, 92, 185

graph, 55–56

multiply, 116–117, 131–145, 151–152, 181–182, 193–196

patterns in, 134

place values in, 40, 41, 187–188

powers of ten, 180, 181

read, 40

relate fractions and, 39–40, 185

  parts of a whole, 39–40

relate to metric lengths, 45–46, 48

round, 53, 149

Secret Code Cards, 41–42D

subtract, 49–50

symmetry around ones place, 41–42D

tenths and hundredths, 39, 41–42D, 181–183

thousandths, 39, 41–42D, 116

word names for, 42A–42D

write, 40, 56

write fractions as, 39

zeros in the product, 134, 148

Denominator, 9–10, 19–20

common, 10, 12, 18, 22, 23

greatest common, 18

Difference. *See* **Subtraction**

Digit-by-Digit, 169–170, 175

Distributive Property, 51–52, 85, 123

Division

adjusting estimate, 169–170

check for reasonable answers, 192, 213

with decimals, 177–179, 181–196

decimals in, 177–190

drawings, 95, 211–212

equations, 209–210

estimation in, 167–170, 213

fractions in, 5–6, 97–102, 184

  unit, 92–94

  word problems with, 97

methods, 163, 184, 192

  adjusted estimate, 169–170

  digit-by-digit, 169–170, 175

  expanded notation, 169–170, 175

of multidigit whole numbers, 163–166

by one-digit divisors, 163–166, 175, 177

real world situations, 96, 171–174, 176, 192

relate multiplication to, 91–94, 180, 183, 193–196

with remainders, 165, 171–174

by two-digit divisors, 167–168, 175, 178

with unit fractions, 92–94

word problems, 96, 97, 176

    write, 212

E

Equation

  fractions and, 86, 209

  situation, 27, 164, 207–210, 289

  solution, 27, 164, 207–210, 228, 289

  solving addition and subtraction equations, 207

  solving equations

    by substitution, 243–244

    two step, 222

    using inverse operations, 91–94

    using order of operations, 221–222, 227

    using parentheses, 221–222, 224

  solving multiplication and division equations, 69–70, 91–94, 122, 152, 173–174, 209

  using a variable to represent an unknown, 247

  writing, 91, 96, 221, 245, 280

Equilateral triangle, 300

Equivalent

  fractions, 3–8, 184, 218

    on a number line, 3–6

Estimate. *See* **Estimation**

Estimation. *See also* **Rounding**

  adjusted, 169–170

  differences, 54

  fractions, 25–26, 214

    use benchmarks, 11, 214

place by place, 167–168

products, 149–150

quotients, 166–170, 213

reasonable answers, 25–26, 54, 142, 166, 192, 208, 210, 213–214

rounding and, 149–150, 213

sums, 54

underestimate, 169

Evaluate, 243–244

Even number, 121–122

Expanded form, 42

Expanded notation

  division, 169–170, 175

  multiplication, 124, 127

Exponent, 119–120, 146–147, 181

Expressions, 245

  definition, 239

  and equations, 287

  evaluating, 243–244

    by substitution, 243–244

    using order of operations, 221–222, 240, 241

  inverse relationships, 91–94, 245

  rules, 245

  simple algebraic, 239

  using parentheses, 42, 51, 242

  using properties, 288

  writing, 239–240, 244, 248, 287

F

Factor, 72, 89

  common, 18

  defined, 72

Family Letter, 1–2, 37–38, 65–66, 111–112, 161–162, 205–206, 237–238, 263–264

Figures, 291. *See also* **Two-dimensional figures**

Focus on Mathematical Practices, **29–30, 57–58, 103–104, 153–154, 197–198, 229–230, 255–256, 301–302**

Foot, 273

Formula
area, 281–284
perimeter, 281–282
volume, 289–290

Fraction bars, 8, 17, 75, 77

Fraction Poster. *See* **Manipulatives**

Fractions
add, 17–18, 25–26, 87, 101–102
area, 76, 84, 282
benchmarks, 11, 214
capacity and, 275
common denominators, 10, 12, 18, 22, 23
commutative property and, 84
comparing, 3, 9–12, 19–20
benchmarks, 11
real world, 77, 87–88
decimal fractions, 92
decimals and, 92, 185
compare and order, 9–12, 87
denominator, 9–10, 19–20
greatest common, 18
least common, 18
unlike, 17, 19–20
as division of whole numbers, 92, 184
division with, 92–102, 184
equations and, 209
equivalent, 3–8, 184, 218
on a number line, 3–6
estimate
to check for reasonableness, 25–26, 214

models, 17, 73, 77
multiplication of, 3–4, 75–80, 83, 97–102, 211, 218
relate to division, 97
non-unit, 71, 75–78
number lines and, 3–6, 74, 280
operations, 83–87, 101–102
compare, 83, 97
summarize, 87, 100
parts and wholes, 3
reading, 40
relate decimals and, 39–40
related to wholes, 3
rename, 17–18, 23
with same denominators, 9
with same numerators but different denominators, 9
simplifying, 3, 5, 21, 22, 79–80
subtract, 19–20, 101–102
benchmarks, 25–26
ungroup, 21, 22
unsimplifying, 3
weight and, 277
benchmarks, 11

G

Gallon, 275

Geometry. *See also* **Measurement**
angle, 250
acute, 250
classify two-dimensional figures, 296–296A, 298
net, 285
polygon, 254, 299–300A, 300C
classify, 296–296A
hexagon, 300
name, 300
octagon, 300

parallelogram, 295–296A

pentagon, 300

quadrilateral, 295–296A, 300

rectangle, 296–296A

regular, 300

rhombus, 295, 296A

sort, 296–296A, 300A, 300C

square, 295, 296A, 300

triangle, 297–298, 300

quadrilaterals, 295–296A, 300

rectangle, 296–296A

   area, 281–284

   sort, 296–296A

rhombus, 295, 296A

triangle, 297–298, 300

   equilateral, 300

Geometry and Measurement Poster.
See **Manipulatives**

Glossary. S14–S24

Gram, 271–272

Graphs

bar

   make a, 56, 230

coordinate plane, 249–252

   distances on, 251–252

   graph points, 250–251, 253–256

line plot, 24, 102, 279–280

ordered pairs, 249–250, 253–254

Greater than, 89

Grouping symbols, 242

braces, 242

brackets, 242

parentheses, 42, 51, 221–222, 242

H

Helping Partners, 11, 41, 44, 58, 178, 191, 221, 224, 248, 250, 285, 290

Hexagon, 300

I

Inverse operations, 245

related equations, 91–94, 180, 183, 193–196, 207–208

situation and solution equations, 27, 164, 207–210

K

Kilogram, 272

L

Least common denominator, 18

Least common multiple, 18

Length, 45–46, 48, 265–268, 273–274, 291–292

Less than, 89

Line plot, 24, 102, 279–280

Liquid Volume, 269–270, 275–276.
See also **Capacity**

M

Manipulatives

Attribute Cards, 300C–300D

centimeter cubes, 285

Decimal Secret Code Cards, 41–42D

fraction bars, 8, 17, 75, 77, 93

Grid Paper (TRB M24), 15, 50, 151

Lined Paper (TRB M64), 50

Lined Paper (TRB M65), 177

Manipulative Kit

   base ten blocks, 113

   Coordinate Plane Poster, 249–250, 252

   Fraction Poster, 5, 76

   Geometry Poster, 299, 300

Place Value Poster, 41, 113, 114

play bills (1-dollar, 10-dollar, 100-dollar), 113–114, 178–179, 181

play coins (pennies, nickels, dimes), 39, 132, 178, 181

pointer, 68

Quadrilateral Hierarchy (TRB M57), 296

MathBoard materials, 3, 75, 93, 103, 113, 115, 154, 197

meter stick, 45, 265

nets for rectangular prisms, 286A–286B

Patterns and Rules (TRB M50), 247

Quadrilateral Cards, 296A–296B

rulers, 250, 295, 297

Thousandths Secret Code Cards, 42A–42D

transparency and overhead projector, 76, 296

Triangle Cards, 298–298B

Two-Dimensional Shape Cards, 300A–300B

unit cube, 285–286

Whole Number Secret Code Cards, 42E–42F

Mass, 271–272. *See also* **Measurement, metric**

Math Drawings, 3, 103, 115, 154, 197

Math Talk

In Activities, 23, 29, 41, 47, 57, 73, 83, 84, 89, 91–93, 100, 103, 123, 125, 131, 163, 181, 187, 194, 197, 227, 229, 239, 252, 253, 255, 272, 281, 291, 299, 301

Math Talk in Action, 13, 16, 55, 142, 192, 226, 266, 273

Measurement

area, 291–292

compare to length and volume, 291–292

formulas for, 281–284

of rectangles, 95, 209, 281–284

customary

capacity, 275–276

fractions and, 275

convert length, 273–274

convert liquid volume, 275–276

convert weight, 277

length, 123, 273–274

solve problems, 274, 276, 278

volume

visualize, 287

weight, 277

ounce, pound, ton, 277

formulas

area, 281–282

perimeter, 281

volume, 289–290

length

compare to area and volume, 123, 291–292

metric

capacity, 269–270

convert length, 265

convert liquid volume, 269–270

convert mass, 271–272

length, 45–46, 48, 265, 291–292

centimeter, 45–46

decimeter, 45–46

dekameter, 46

meter, 265

millimeter, 265

liquid volume. *See* Capacity

mass, 271–272

kilogram, 272

perimeter, 281

calculate, 273

formulas for, 281

of rectangles, 281

of squares, 283

relate area, length, and volume, 291–292

volume, 285–288
    capacity and, 275
    compare to area and length, 291–292
    formula, 289–290

Mental math
    addition and subtraction using, 29, 215
    check solutions using, 166
    comparison using, 215
    division and multiplication using, 166, 191, 213

Meter, 265

Metric measurement.
See **Measurement, metric**

Millimeter, 45–46, 265

Misleading language, 215–216

Mixed number
    add and subtract with, 15–16, 22, 24
    improper fractions and, 13–14
    multiplication of, 81–82
    represent, 13

Models
    area, 76, 77, 81, 84, 128
    array, 123, 128
    break-apart, 207–208
    comparison bars, 219
    fraction bars, 8, 17, 75, 77
    number line, 74
    rectangle, 81, 82, 128, 209

Money, 197–198
    adding, 47–48
    division of, 177, 179, 192
    fractions of dollars, 43, 181–182
    multiplication of, 131–132, 135–137
        place shifts in, 113–117, 135–137, 145–148, 181
    pattern shifts in, 113–117, 135–140, 145–148, 181–182

Multiples
    common, 17–18

Multiplication
    comparisons, 68–70, 89, 216, 217–218
        with bars, 68
        with whole numbers and decimals, 145
    concepts, 67–70
    decimal, 131–145, 151–152, 193–196
    decimal places in a product, 131, 148
    estimation, 149–150
    factor. *See* Factor
    fractions in, 3–4, 72, 87, 97–102, 211, 218
        compare to addition, 83
        non-unit, 71, 74
        strategies, 79–80
        unit, 67, 73
        visualize, 71
    grouping situations, 221
    methods, 123–128
        expanded notation, 124, 127
        place value sections (area model), 76, 81, 84, 128, 209
        related equations, 91–94, 180, 183
        shortcut, 126–127
        simplify and, 79
    mixed numbers, 81–82
    of money, 113–117, 131–132, 135–137
    patterns
        with fives, 121–122
        shift, 134, 135–140, 145–148, 181–182
        with zeros and ones, 118, 134
    products, 72, 73, 89, 118, 121, 131, 148
        estimating and rounding, 149–150
    properties
        Associative, 85, 143–144, 288, 289
        Commutative, 84, 98, 143–144, 288, 289
        Distributive, 85, 123

real world word problems, 51, 77,
129–130, 142

relate division and, 91–94, 180, 183,
193–196

situation and solution equations, 164,
209–210, 289

strategies, 79–80

with tens, hundreds, and thousands,
116–120, 145

with tenths, hundredths, and
thousandths (0.1, 0.01, and 0.001),
116, 131–134, 138–141

of two-digit numbers, 125–128

with unit fractions, 67, 73

use parenthesis in, 42, 221

word problems
solve, 78, 79–80, 82, 90, 97, 152
write, 211–212

write equations, 96, 221

with zeros, 118

Multiplication methods, 123–124

expanded notation, 124, 127

rectangle sections (area model), 81, 209

related equations, 91–94, 180, 183

shortcut, 126–127

simplify and multiply, 79

Multiplication table, 7

Multiplier, 145

**Multistep problems, 28, 225–228, 268,
270, 272, 274, 278**

Non-unit fraction, 71, 74

Number line

decimals on, 53

distance between numbers on, 71, 251

fractions on, 43, 74
equivalent, 3–6

Numbers

add, 47–48

compare, 44

decimal
symmetry around ones place, 41–42D

even, 121–122

graph, 55–56

prime, 248

round
estimate and, 149–150, 213

scale, 55

visualize, 43, 71

Numerator, 9

Octagon, 300

One-dimensional figures, 291

Order

decimals, 56

Ordered pairs, 249–250

graph, 253–254

Order of operations, 221–222, 227, 240

Parallel, 296A

Parallelogram, 295–296A

Parentheses, 42, 51, 221–222, 242

Partial products, 123, 141–144

Path to Fluency, 128, 129

Patterns, 245–248

decimal, 134, 179, 187–188

form ordered pairs, 246

© Houghton Mifflin Harcourt Publishing Company

fraction, 75

generate, 245–246, 253

graphs and, 253–254

identify relationships, 104, 245–247, 302

numerical, 245–247, 253–254

with products, 148

with zeros, 118, 134, 179

Perimeter

calculate, 273

formulas, 281–282

of rectangles, 281–284

of squares, 283

Place value, 40, 41, 187–188

Place Value Poster. *See* **Manipulatives**

Place Value Sections method of multiplication, 123, 127

Points, graphing of, 250–251, 253–256

Points on a coordinate plane, 249–256

Polygon. *See* **Geometry, polygon**

Pound, 277

Prime number, 248

Predict, 89–90, 98–101, 195, 214

Problem Solving

all operations, 221–224

decimals, 142

fractions, 27–28, 101–102

hidden information, 266–267

multistep, 28, 225–228, 268, 270, 272, 274, 278

situation equation, 27, 164, 207–210, 289

solution equation, 27, 164, 207–210, 228, 289

strategies, 214

Solve a Simpler Problem, 197

too little information, 223–224

too much information, 223–224

two step, 222

types, S5–S9

writing problems, 211–212

Product. *See* **Multiplication, products**

Properties

Associative

of addition, 51–52

of multiplication, 85, 143–144, 288, 289

Commutative

of addition, 52

of multiplication, 84, 98, 143–144, 288, 289

Distributive, 51–52, 85, 123, 143–144

Puzzled Penguin, 8, 14, 16, 26, 47, 49, 55, 80, 87, 100, 121, 136, 144, 147, 174, 184, 228, 242, 252, 267, 286

Q

Quadrilateral, 295–296A, 300

Quadrilateral Cards, 296A–296B

R

Reasonable answers, 25–26, 54, 142, 166, 192, 208, 210, 213–214

Rectangle, 296–296A

area, 95, 209, 281–284

Remainders, 165, 171–174, 270

Rhombus, 295, 296A

Rounding

decimals, 53, 149

estimate differences, 54

estimate products, 149–150

estimate sums, 54

graphs and, 55

scales and, 55

S

Scale

graph, 55, 254

rounding units on graphs, 55

Scaling (multiplication), 218

predict the product, 89–90, 98–100

Secret Code Cards

decimals, 41–42D, 44

whole numbers, 42E–42F

Shift patterns in division

decimal amounts, 180, 181–183, 187–190

Shift patterns in multiplication, 113–120, 145–148

decimal amounts, 116–117, 135–140, 181–182

with powers of ten, 119–120, 146–147

whole numbers, 113–115, 119–120

with zeros, 118, 134

Shortcut method of multiplication, 126–127

Simplify, 79–80, 241

an expression, 241–242

a fraction, 3, 5, 21, 22, 79–80

Situation equation, 27, 164, 207–210, 289

Solution equations, 27, 164, 207–210

Solve a Simpler Problem, 197

Sorting rules, 298

Square, 295, 296A, 300

Square unit, 123

Subtraction

of decimals and whole numbers, 49–50

estimate differences, 54

of fractions, 19–20, 25–26, 87, 101–102

methods, 21

ungroup left to right, 49

ungroup right to left, 49

of mixed numbers, 16, 22, 24

relate to addition, 207–208

ungrouping, 22, 49–50

Symmetry

around ones place, 41–42D

T

Technology

Destination Math, In every TE Lesson

Personal Math Trainer, In every TE Lesson

Whiteboard, In every TE Lesson

Term, defined, 245–246, 253

Thousands, 41–42D, 116

Thousandths, 39, 41–42D, 43, 116

Too little information, 223–224

Too much information, 223–224

Triangle, 297–298, 300

equilateral, 300

Triangle Cards, 298–298B

Two-dimensional figures, 291, 299–300A, 300C

closed, 299

concave, 299

convex, 299

hexagon, 300

octagon, 300

open, 299

parallelogram, 295–296A

pentagon, 300

rectangle, 95, 209, 281–284, 296–296A

regular polygon, 300

rhombus, 295, 296A

sort, 296–296A, 298, 300A, 300C

square, 295, 296A, 300

triangle, 297–298, 300

Two-Dimensional Shape Cards, 300A–300B

U

Underestimate, 169

Ungroup, 21, 22, 49–50

Unit

converting, 265, 269–272

cube, 285–287, 289

Unit fraction, 67, 73, 92–94

Unit Review/Test, 31–36, 59–64, 105–110, 155–160, 199–204, 231–236, 257–262, 303–308

Unsimplify, 3

V

Variable, 239, 243, 247

Venn diagram, 298

Vertex, 250

Vocabulary Activities , S10–S13

Volume, 285–288, 293–294

build rectangular prisms, 285

composite figure, 293–294

count cubes, 285–286

count layers, 287

formula, 289–290

of rectangular prism, 285–290, 293–294

visualize, 287

W

Weight, 271, 277–278

What's the Error?, 8, 14, 16, 25–26, 80, 100, 136, 143–144, 147, 174, 183, 252, 267, 286, 300A, 300C. *See also* **Puzzled Penguin**

Width, 123, 281

Word problem. *See* **Problem solving**

Write word problems, 152, 211–212

X

x-axis, 249–256

x-coordinate, 249–256

Y

Yard, 273

y-axis, 249–256

y-coordinate, 249–256

Z

Zeros in a product, 118, 121, 148

Zeros patterns, 118, 134, 179

© Houghton Mifflin Harcourt Publishing Company

Glossary **S45**